# Issues of Faith and Morals

ARCHBISHOP GEORGE PELL

# Issues of Faith and Morals

Ignatius Press

San Francisco

This edition of *Issues of Faith and Morals*
is published by arrangement with
Oxford University Press, Australia.

Printed in 1997, 1999 by Ignatius Press, San Francisco
© George Pell 1996
All rights reserved
ISBN 0–89870–634–3
Library of Congress catalogue number 97–70813
Printed in the United States of America ∞

# Contents

# Preface

*Issues of Faith and Morals* was written to spread knowledge and understanding of the one true God and to explain the basic truths at the heart of the good life. My ambition is to strengthen the hope of young people, especially those in their senior years at Catholic secondary schools, by explaining to them something of God's goodness and love as revealed in the Catholic tradition, which is ancient yet ever new. This book is designed to encourage young people in a sincere search for truth, recognizing that their individual journeys are many and various. It presents and attempts to explain Christian alternatives to the conventions that assail us in the media and in advertising today. This book encourages students to examine some important contemporary issues from a Catholic perspective and to consider some of the basic questions that have troubled philosophers and saints throughout history. Is there a God? What is the purpose of existence? What makes actions good or evil? Is there life after death? My hope is that at least some students will be stimulated, even provoked, to enquire more deeply and to read further on some of these problems.

The religious teachings of this volume are mainstream Catholic, taken from the *Catechism of the Catholic Church*, which appeared in English translation in June 1994. This magnificent summary of Catholic teaching, the fruit of many years of work by an international commission, has been given to us by Pope John Paul II as "a sure norm for teaching the faith and thus a valid and legitimate instrument for ecclesiastical communion". It remains the essential database, the springboard for Catholic religious education, a handy court of appeal for the arguments and discussions on what the Catholic Church officially teaches. The Holy Father also explained in his Apostolic Constitution that the Catechism "is meant to encourage and assist in the writing of new local catechisms, which take into account various situations and cultures, while carefully preserving the unity of faith and fidelity to Catholic doctrine".

*Issues of Faith and Morals* is not a catechism and does not set out to give a comprehensive coverage of the essentials of Catholic doctrine. But it is an explicit attempt to marry some contemporary concerns with Catholic doctrines; to teach the same unique Christian truths in a way that is comprehensible, perhaps even attractive, to educated young people. It is an attempt to evoke the romance of orthodoxy (G. K. Chesterton's phrase), an appeal to that "pattern of sound teaching" that Saint Paul commended to Titus: "Keep as your pattern the sound teaching you have heard from me, in the faith and love that are in Christ Jesus. You have been trusted to look after something precious; guard it with the help of the Holy Spirit who lives in us" (2 Timothy 1:13–14).

The book is not an explicit call to conversion of heart or mind; therefore, it is not like a sermon or a retreat or a parish mission. It is, rather, a series of doctrinal explanations, expressly designed to provoke thought, questions and discussion. It makes an appeal to the criterion of truth: to use this book, readers have to think and reason. It calls students to discover for themselves the life-giving truths at the heart of the tradition, which are often obscured by routine and by long-term acquaintance and, increasingly today, by a simple ignorance of the tradition.

It is my conviction that ideas are powerful in the long term, even when they are sometimes rejected in the short term. Saint Paul started off by persecuting the Christians, being present at the stoning of the first martyr, Saint Stephen. Nevertheless, he became the greatest missionary and theologian of the New Testament period.

This book is a clear-cut rejection of the anti-intellectual traditions so dear to many. All Catholics, especially young Catholics, have a right to know what constitutes Catholic teaching, especially if they find themselves unable to accept particular doctrines. Many of those drifting away from religious practice have few clear ideas of what they are abandoning. Many of those with problems of faith and belief may imagine that their difficulties are new, or even unique. Knowledge of itself is not enough for faith or for living a

● ● ● ● ● ● ● ● ● ● ● ● ● ● ● ● ● ● ● ● ● ● ● ● ● ● ● ● ● ● ● ● ● ● ● ● ●

good life, but it is one essential constituent if an educated person is to continue as a believer. An adult understanding of Catholicism means that a person is better equipped to return after drifting away. Many drifters do return when they decide to marry or when they have to decide what values to pass on to their children. An adult understanding also means, most importantly of all, that a believer is better placed to survive life's difficulties.

For all these reasons, many sections of this book are like introductory theology classes, sometimes with a dose of philosophy included. They can be read, thought about and discussed by atheists, agnostics, doubters, the muddled and strong believers. I repeat that this book is not an explicit call to conversion, but an attempt to develop understanding and knowledge. With God's grace, the right circumstances and the appropriate personal decisions, conversion might or might not come at some other time. I recognize that a percentage of students in every class are indifferent, some hostile. My task here is to inform and to present the full Catholic teaching, but not to browbeat or to indoctrinate.

The book is also written with the conviction that nothing is to be gained by hiding the severity of Christ's teaching. Such a concealment would be unfair to readers and has proved disastrous in practice. The "sweetening" of Christianity produces spectators, not joiners, because the strength of the Church lies in the Cross as the necessary prelude to the Resurrection. And we have our Savior's promise that "my yoke is easy and my burden light."

On some topics, excerpts from poems and literature have been quoted or recommended for examination and discussion. There are many other possibilities for teachers and students to use, drawing on their own experiences. A number of pieces of music have also been suggested. Ten or fifteen minutes of such music could make a welcome difference in the religious education routine and might provoke lively discussion and many differences of opinion. Naturally, I believe strongly in the importance of religious commitment for every person, which in turn affects the well-being of communities, even though I am not directly working for that in this book. Therefore, I hope and pray that in some cases, at least, these few words will form part of a mosaic, with personal exam-

ple, prayer, service and community spirit to help people choose
Christ and the Catholic tradition. My prayer is expressed in the
words of the great Australian poet James McAuley (1917–1976):

> It's easy said—I wish my words might chime
> With fitting deeds as easy as they rhyme,
> Yet somehow, between prayer and common sense,
> Hearts may be touched, and lives have influence.
> And when the heart is once disposed to see,
> Then reason can unlock faith's treasury.

# Source Acknowledgments

The author and publisher are grateful to copyright holders for granting permission to reproduce copyright material in this book. Copyright details are as follows:

Jack Chalker for the watercolor of "Weary" Dunlop operating in a jungle hospital, p. 1;

Bruce Dawe and Longman Cheshire for the poems "Husband and Wife", p. 52, and "The Sticking Point", p. 138;

Jeff Hook for the cartoon on p. 164;

*Madonna of the Magnificat* (detail), 1482, by Botticelli, p. 107;

Right to Life, Victoria, p. 129;

Tony Maskell Photography, pp. 33, 43, 55, 63, 75, 87, 119, 141.


Every effort has been made to trace the original source of material used in this book. Where the attempt has been unsuccessful, the author and publisher would be pleased to hear from the copyright holders in order to rectify any errors or omissions.

# Author Acknowledgments

Many friends and acquaintances cooperated to advise on *Issues of Faith and Morals*. An immense debt of gratitude is due first of all to Mary Helen Woods, not only for her chapter, but also for her invaluable advice, enthusiasm and assistance on every aspect of this work. The Thomas More Centre distributed nine of these chapters as individual broadsheets, obtaining valuable feedback on sales of between 10,000 to 50,000 copies per sheet. These sales encouraged me to print this collection.

Each chapter was tested in the senior classes of two schools. Special thanks to Mr. Tom Kendall, Principal of Sacred Heart College (for girls) at Oakleigh in Melbourne, and his students and teachers, and to Br. Quentin, F.S.C., Principal of St. Bede's College (for boys), Mentone in Melbourne, and his students and teachers. The comments were always honest, sometimes encouraging, sometimes critical. They provoked substantial revisions.

Tony Maskell produced most of the beautiful photos, my sister Margaret Pell was the principal source of advice on the music chosen, and Dr. Gerald Fogarty and Tom Razga were my chief advisers on medical matters. John Casamento and Br. Don Gallagher, C.F.C., also provided photos.

The following people contributed valuable advice on one or more chapters: Michael and Ruth Casey, Karin Clark, Christy Collins, Rev. Dr. Peter Cross, Sr. Mary Dalton (R.I.P.), Rev. Dr. Gerard Diamond, Monsignor Peter Elliott, Phil Glendinning, Fr. D. J. Hart, Rev. Dr. John Honner, S.J., Rev. Dr. Tony Kelly, C.Ss.R., Steve and Anne Lawrence, Anne McFarlane, Anne McIlroy, Professor Gabrielle McMullen, Tim and Catrina O'Leary, Sarah Pell, Fr. Charlie Portelli, Terri Thrower, Fr. John Walshe and the Woods family. Occasionally they obtained further advice from friends of theirs.

To all of them, my thanks. Any errors of fact and judgment are my own.

# CHAPTER ONE

# Right or Wrong?

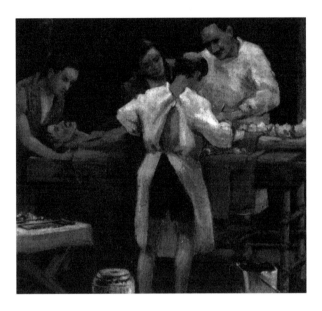

*Most people agree in many cases about what is right and wrong. On other issues, there are big differences of opinion. How do we recognize the truth?*

The well-loved comic book character Charlie Brown, who began his career in the 1960s, once claimed that it didn't matter what you believed as long as you were sincere. Was he right?

Many people are still tempted to agree with Charlie; certainly, some of our beliefs have few consequences for ourselves or others. But to assume that beliefs in the areas of faith and morals do not matter is dangerous and mistaken. Immense consequences follow from some beliefs. A few examples will suffice to show this.

Do heaven and hell exist? Does God reward the good and punish the evil? Is political violence and bloodshed an appropriate way of resolving political differences? Is abortion acceptable? Is adultery permitted sometimes, regularly or never? It does matter what we believe on issues such as these.

Important consequences often follow when we act on our beliefs, consequences important to us and to other people. Therefore, while sincerity is good and necessary, it is rarely enough by itself. Something more is needed. Hitler, Stalin and Pol Pot were probably sincere. Were they right? Were their actions justified? Unless adults stand for something, they will fall for anything. To function well, society and the Church need people of integrity.


**Honest Differences**

In society today, there is much confusion and many conflicting opinions. How is it possible to know what is right and what is wrong?

Catholics and all "mainstream" Christians believe that Jesus Christ, the Son of God, is "the way, the truth and the life" (John 14:6) because he is "the image of the invisible God" (Colossians 1:15). Therefore, Jesus' religious and moral teachings have a unique authority: they contain the answers to what makes a life good and what constitutes a good person. The authority of the Catholic Church and the self-confidence that enables her to stand against the tide of public opinion come from the fact that she restates and develops the teachings of Christ, who is the voice of truth about good and evil.

This bald claim to moral truths, namely, that moral matters are not decided by force, opinion polls or sentiment and that morality is not a human invention but comes from God, is a crucial point of difference between religious and secular people. Jesus' moral teaching is based on two great commandments: love of God and love of neighbor (Luke 10:25–27). All the teaching of the law and the prophets depends on this double base (Matthew 22:40). Genuine love of God, spelled out in the first three of the Ten Commandments, is not possible without keeping the other seven commandments, which specify the love of our neighbors. As Saint John explained, "he who does not love his brother whom

2

he has seen, cannot love God whom he has not seen" (1 John 4:20). Another focus of our Lord's moral teaching is found in the Beatitudes (Matthew 5:3–12). These complement the Commandments, describing the attitudes and dispositions that lead to eternal life. They are, above all, promises, descriptions of the values of heaven and invitations to a closer communion of life with Christ.

## The Power of Reason

To arrive at moral truths according to the teaching of Christ implies that we have faith in his wisdom and his divine status. Even to believers, such a way of reasoning could seem like a form of rigid fundamentalism (i.e., an absolute appeal to authority with little regard for reason). What about people who are unsure of their faith? Is there any room for human reason?

The Catholic Church has a long tradition of reasoning in both moral philosophy and moral theology, which has been developed through many centuries. Right from her earliest years, the Church has encouraged people to think and to use their intelligence to help solve human and religious problems. For example, we now recognize much better than in previous centuries that there are laws of hygiene and sanitation that must be followed to avoid infection and disease. We also accept that certain ecological laws must be respected if we are to avoid degrading or damaging the environment.

In moral matters, there is also a natural law reflecting God's eternal law, which is recognized by our reason, our real but imperfect capacity to distinguish good from evil. This natural law embodies a respect for the dignity of every person and for human rights (many of which are now recognized in the United Nations Charter).

Sometimes, people without faith in God will be strong defenders of Christian morality because they recognize the many good values that Christian morality protects. Christians often say that we use our consciences to work out the right thing to do.

## Conscience

Conscience is an awareness of moral truth. A grown-up person recognizes that morality is defined by what is humanly good and reasonable. This is another way of describing our Lord's moral teachings. The Commandments are not obstacles designed to make life difficult; nor are they there to test us, to distinguish the strong from the weak. The Commandments are there to protect us and to protect what is good in human life.

In the broadest sense, conscience is our instinctive and natural grasping, our understanding of basic moral principles. Both reason and feelings are usually involved. Some people, for instance, feel sick when they see an act of violence; if the violence is horrific enough, people can go into deep shock. More particularly, we exercise our conscience to decide what should be done in a particular case. Is this action in conformity with the law of God? Is it wrong from natural law?

We should distinguish our conscience from our feelings and instincts (conscious and subconscious). A sensitive adult moral conscience develops from this process and is refined by reason, good example and the love of other people. Saint Paul told us that everyone has to struggle to be good—even saints have evil impulses, which they can control but cannot entirely remove.

In good people, reason and instincts are usually on the same wavelength, but because of our tendency to sin, this is not always the case: a gossiper can feel virtuous after destroying someone's good name; a psychopath can inflict terrible injuries on another and feel no remorse at all. In matters of sexual morality, our feelings can be notoriously unreliable.

A good moral understanding is not the same as social conventions because a good conscience uses reason and is based ultimately on moral principles. Social conventions are often good because they embody the moral traditions of our ancestors, but they are also unreliable—for example, racial prejudice is sometimes an old tradition.

It is common for some people to view Christian or Church teachings as another type of social convention. But basic Christian moral teaching goes beyond convention. Some people want the

Church to change her teachings, especially in matters of sexuality, but the Church does not have the power to change the morals that Christ taught. Therefore, basic moral teachings cannot be changed, even when they are very difficult to follow, such as the teachings that we must forgive our enemies and that sexual activities must be confined to marriage. But peace often comes from doing the right thing or, if we fail in this, from believing in the reality of God's forgiveness, then asking for and receiving that forgiveness.

The proficiency of our conscience, our capacity for accurate moral judgment, can improve or decline as our spiritual sight strengthens or weakens. As Jesus explained, "The eye is the lamp of the body. So if your eye is sound, your whole body will be full of light" (Matthew 6:22). With increasing age and education, and especially through prayer and upright actions, our moral wisdom should increase. But unfortunately, this does not always happen, as human development can result in an improved capacity to deceive ourselves.

**Primacy of Truth**

From 1962 to 1965, Pope John XXIII convened a meeting called the Second Vatican Council that aimed to renew and reform the Church. Some claim that since the Second Vatican Council, Catholics are now allowed to follow their individual consciences, even if this means going against the teachings of Christ and the Church. In Western countries, there is much confusion about morality and about notions of right and wrong. This confusion is now strong within the Catholic community too.

In 1993, Pope John Paul II issued an encyclical (teaching letter) on moral matters entitled *Veritatis Splendor* (in English, *The Splendor of the Truth*). It received a lot of coverage in the media, and many Catholics and even some non-Catholics welcomed it. It was also strongly attacked. In this encyclical, the Pope officially recognized a crisis that the Church is facing: namely, that even the most fundamental Christian moral teachings are being attacked or ignored. Mistaken ideas about conscience are often at the heart of this crisis.

Some claim that our individual consciences are free and that we are free to make up our own minds about what is right and wrong. Does this make sense? Are we free to hurt others? You might as well say we are free to set our watches at the wrong time. A few minutes off generally does not matter much; however, if one's watch is hours off, disaster can follow. We are not free to do the wrong thing.

Some mistakenly speak of "the primacy of conscience"; others are a bit more careful and speak of "the primacy of informed conscience". This means that the Catholic who has studied the matter is entitled to contradict Christ and the Church. Such claims are quite mistaken. We do speak of the primacy of the pope. We could usefully speak of the primacy of truth or the primacy of the word of God in Scriptures, but to speak of the primacy of conscience is at best a misleading half-truth.

In matters of belief and morals, there is no substitute for an honest and freely given consent. Such a consent is necessary but not sufficient. Sincerity is not enough, although it is needed. The Pope says that conscience is "the proximate norm of personal morality", but it is not the supreme tribunal. Sincerity is needed, but sincere people can be mistaken. Conscience is like a compass used to find our way. If the compass is out of kilter, we will be mistaken about our route. In other words, one's conscience cannot have the last word, because conscience is at the service of truth. We use our conscience to work out what should be done, but we could be mistaken. We are only free to seek the truth or to sin. A sincerely held belief does not entitle us to violate the rights of others or to deny the moral teachings of Christ.

There are many opportunities for people to exercise their consciences; life is often complicated. However, there are also many occasions where the issues of right and wrong are clear-cut—then we need God's help and a dose of moral courage. Christ our Lord explains life as it truly is. Some actions are wonderfully right; others are horribly cruel and wrong. Life is not a gray fog of uncertainty and unhappiness. The truth really does set us free.

## Moral Blindness or Honest Mistakes?

Ignorance of the law is no defense if we are prosecuted before a judge or magistrate. Is God like this, or can we make an honest mistake? God judges what is in our hearts. He is not limited to appearances or concerned only with public order. Therefore, God does not hold us guilty for honest mistakes. Committing a sin is not like breaking a taboo, because to sin, we have to know what we are doing. Nevertheless, moral blindness is possible. If we do not want to know the truth or refuse to make an effort to find out the facts, then God will hold us responsible for the consequent mistakes. Moral blindness can produce the worst crimes. Hardened sinners (for example, killers) can lose all moral sensibility.

## Too Hard or Too Soft

The Catholic Church is often attacked for being too strict, just as she is also attacked for being too soft on unpopular sinners. This is because the Church teaches that all sins and crimes can be forgiven by Christ via the Church (if the sinner repents) and because she clearly spells out moral principles.

In relation to morals, the Church has two important roles: she has to set out ideals and norms and articulate them through principles and prohibitions, while at the same time offering ways to deal with human weakness. Trouble emerges when these two different roles are confused. Christ and the Church distinguish the sin from the sinner and the crime from the criminal. We are urged to love sinners and to hate sin. In this sense, the Church is both merciful and severe.

An important rule of life, although something of a paradox, is that the happiest individuals and communities are disciplined when love and joy are protected by rules or commandments. Most students prefer to be at a school that has good morale and discipline, where the teachers are competent and just, and where the rules are accepted and followed. There can be more love, fun and happiness in families where parents and children know their roles and do their best, however imperfectly. Students have to study to pass examinations, athletes must train hard to excel at sports. The Commandments are like the rules of the game, like a highway through the countryside of life. They are real limits, followed at some cost to bring joy and freedom.

Our Lord required his disciples to renounce themselves and take up the cross if they wanted to follow him (Matthew 16:24), but he also promised that those who labored would find their yokes to be easy and the burden light. Christ promises rest for our souls, especially when we are troubled (Matthew 11:28–30). Two thousand years of history have proven Christ right on both counts.

• • • • • • • • • • • • • • • • • • • • • • • • • •

*Bibliography*

*Catechism of the Catholic Church*, pt. 3, chaps. 1 and 2, pars. 1691–1948.
Pope John Paul II, *Evangelium Vitae* (1994).
Pope John Paul II, *Veritatis Splendor* (1993).

*For Review*

1. What makes an action right or wrong?

2. Are we free to do whatever we like?

3. What is conscience and how does it operate?

*Consider These*

1. How does one find out what is good and what is evil?

2. "There is no absolute right and no absolute wrong." Where do atrocities like the Nazi Holocaust or Soviet Gulag fit into your moral scheme?

3. "Doing the right thing is harder in the short run but easier in the long run than doing the wrong thing." Is this true? Give an example.

4. Describe a situation where it was difficult to work out what was the right thing to do.

5. Sometimes we rationalize the fact that we have made a wrong decision. Give an example of how this might happen.

6. What is the role of the Catholic Church in establishing a set of principles by which one may lead one's life?

*Extension Exercises*

1. Some music can express the spirit of evil. The short orchestral work *The Warriors,* written by the Australian composer Percy Grainger (1882–1961), is one such piece. The Soviet composer Dmitry Shostakovich (1906–1975) lived all his adult life under communist dictatorship. His Seventh (Leningrad) Symphony

was written ostensibly to portray the sufferings of the Russian people under Nazi attack. A deeper intention was to express the suffering under the leadership of Joseph Stalin, who was responsible for more deaths than Hitler. The music is powerful, grim, foreboding and oppressive. What piece of music best expresses for you the spirit of evil?

2. What piece of music best expresses the spirit of goodness? What about the opening of the Fifth Symphony by Ludwig van Beethoven (1770–1827), which the Allies chose as their theme for the victorious landings in Normandy against the Nazis? Can you suggest any others?

3. "If you were to destroy in mankind the belief in immortality, not only love but every living force maintaining the life of the world would at once be dried up. Moreover, nothing then would be immoral; everything would be permissible, even cannibalism." These words were written by the Russian writer Fedor Dostoyevsky (1821–1881). Do you agree that heaven and hell are as important in moral matters as Dostoyevsky claims?

4. King Henry VIII of England (1491–1547) denied the religious leadership of the pope and declared himself head of the Church of England. This provoked a great struggle. Robert Bolt's play *A Man for All Seasons,* also made into a film, describes the final days of Sir Thomas More (1478–1535), Lord Chancellor of England and now a Catholic saint, who was executed by King Henry because he refused to deny the pope's authority.

   a. What is the role of conscience in *A Man for All Seasons*?

   b. Is it reasonable for a person to die for his principles?

   c. Would Thomas More have said that he died for the sake of his conscience or for truth and for the Church? Is there any difference?

5. The following poem, titled "In the Vestibule", was written by Australian poet Bruce Dawe as a response to a doctor's admission that he had performed abortions up until six months of pregnancy.

Above the clinic entrance, words of fire,
which burned our eyes on entering, boldly said:
*Blind hope and desperation here conspire* . . .

Here, too a ghostly plenitude of dead,
who died because they were not suffered birth
—some, at the very brink of being, sped

Clear of the barbed entanglements of earth,
while others lived five months or even more
(slept, woke, kicked at times, heard music, mirth)

Before being hustled off . . . We turned and saw
within that place a surgeon whose dark skill
it was to do the hustling. He wore

A green gown, and his specialism was to kill
by puncturing infant skulls and diligently
suctioning out the brains. We stood stock-still,

Shaken by cries the world would never hear,
from those forbidden voices by decree
(the cost of living proving far too dear).

Returning from that nether-region, still
those cries pursued us: endless, indignant, shrill.


What evil is Dawe describing so powerfully? Do you share his immense indignation? What other actions would you condemn strongly?

# CHAPTER TWO

# Is Jesus the Way, the Truth and the Life?

*This splendid mosaic of Christ is from the twelfth-century Norman cathedral in Cefalù, Sicily. Is it representative of your idea of Jesus?*

In the last chapter, we looked at concepts of right and wrong. But how are we making these judgments? Where does our conscience come from? Who was Jesus, and can he still teach us?

## Christians

A Christian accepts that Jesus Christ is Lord and the Son of the one true God, and he is expected to follow Christ's teachings, however imperfectly. Catholics, Orthodox, Anglicans and Protestants are all Christian. A Christian needs to make an act of faith to say "I believe."

Christians should be not only believers but good people, even though many are sinners while retaining their faith. Also, many good people follow other religions, such as Judaism, Islam and Buddhism. Sometimes, good people have no religion.

Jesus Christ is the son of Mary as well as the Son of God. He is the second Divine Person of the Blessed Trinity, who existed from all eternity before he became a man. This preexistence is not a metaphor or some psychological ideal but an everlasting reality, part of the supreme divine mystery. As true God and true man, Jesus was able to redeem and save us. As the Son of God, his teachings on faith and morals have a unique authority.

Through Jesus, God visited his chosen people, the Jews, fulfilling the promise made to their father Abraham. Billions of people have followed Christ's teachings over nearly two thousand years, and tens of thousands of people called martyrs have died for his cause, many of them in this century.

In Hebrew, the word "Jesus" means "God saves". "Christ" is not a family name but comes from the Greek translation of the Hebrew word "Messiah", which means "Anointed".

## Need for Religion

Some people claim that everyone is going in the same direction. A few even claim that religious beliefs are not necessary or useful. However, history shows that we are not all going in the same direction. Some people are systematically and repeatedly evil. Still others have a very different idea of right and wrong. A few people deny that the one true God exists; many more, although still a minority, ignore God most of the time and live as though he did not exist. Sadly, some despair, thinking life has no meaning. Such despair can sometimes lead to suicide, even among young people.

To maintain integrity, each person has to seek the truth honestly; in daily life, each person regularly chooses between good and evil. Everyone encounters suffering at some stage. People answer these challenges in different ways. The truth about things can be a great support.

In other words, everyone needs a purpose in life, beyond selfishness; something to live for. Unless we stand for something, we could fall for anything. High principles even provide reasons for which heroes will die.

As the only Son of God, the second Person of the Blessed Trinity, Jesus is God's special messenger to us, who "revealed" to us the basic truths of life. His teachings have a unique authority, giving us certainty where human intelligence could only indicate probabilities. He confirmed to us that God is good and interested in us and that a life of reward or punishment lies beyond the grave for everyone.

However, Jesus is not just a philosopher giving us inside information on the state of things; he also brings us the Maker's instructions on how life is to be lived: "Come, follow me" (Matthew 4:18–20).

Jesus Christ, our Lord, is the one mediator between God and man, because he is both God and man. Neither Muhammad nor Buddha claimed to be divine. Muhammad bore eloquent witness to the one true God and claimed to be a prophet. Buddha, the enlightened one, taught many beautiful truths about life but left God out of the discussion.

## Jesus' Life Story

Many people feel that they know the basic facts of Jesus' life and are not much interested in going farther. Sometimes, our small store of religious knowledge serves to immunize us against catching the "real thing"! When we are given the full picture, Jesus' teaching and his life story are both disturbing and baffling.

We still date history from the year in which Jesus was born, for example, A.D. 1997 (Anno Domini, which means "In the year of our Lord"). But because of erroneous calculations, he might actually have been born about 4 or 5 B.C. (before Christ)!

Jesus was born in Bethlehem and lived for thirty years in a small village called Nazareth before he embarked on a public life of about three years' duration. To our disappointment, the Gospels tell us little about his early years, his working life or the formative influences on him. Nothing is known of Jesus' physical appearance, but no one followed him for his face!

Jesus did not come from a rich or aristocratic background. His mother, Mary, was a young Jewish girl and her husband, Joseph, whom tradition describes as an older man, was a carpenter. Born in a stable, his background was not only poor but also suspicious, as he was suspected of illegitimacy. Unlike Saint Paul, who studied theology under the famous Rabbi Gamaliel in Jerusalem, Jesus did not have the advantages of a first-class formal education. We are not even sure that he could write; certainly he left us no writings of his own.

His public career as a religious leader was short, spectacular and ruthlessly terminated. He did not work in the centers of power and influence but usually among the poor in Palestine, which was one of the least prosperous outposts of the Roman Empire. The area was also the site of regular political unrest, something like northern Ireland this century. The Romans brutally suppressed armed rebellions in Palestine in A.D. 66–70 and in A.D. 135. A wonderful and provocative storyteller, he was also a miracle worker, curing the sick, the disturbed, the possessed, and sometimes even bringing the dead to life.

He mixed with "criminal" types such as thieves, tax collectors and prostitutes, while simultaneously and successfully making his fantastic claim to sinlessness. He was no pious jellyfish: for example, he drove the money changers from the temple, an awesome scene captured wonderfully by the painter El Greco.

He was the cause of profound divisions, provoking the fanatical hostility of some Pharisees. The Geresene people asked him to leave them (after their pigs charged over the cliff to destruction), while even his home-town people on one occasion wanted to stone him. Mark the evangelist tells us that some of Jesus' own family thought that Jesus was mad. He was eventually condemned, scourged and crucified.

Jesus' triumphs and his friends and his followers were real, but his public life was a mix of love and hate, support and opposition, wonderful moments and hurtful disappointments.

His end was sad, with Judas, one of the twelve apostles, betraying him to his enemies. He died in Jerusalem on Mount Calvary, between two thieves, abandoned by most of his followers. Of the men, only the apostle John stayed with him, while Peter, the leader and the "rock man", denied him three times. More of his women followers stayed with him. Three days after his crucifixion, Jesus rose triumphant from the tomb.

Our Lord had no public relations experts to give him a "good image" and no mass media to spread his message. Yet, even during his life, people came by the thousands to see and hear him; young and old, rich and poor, and especially the outcasts, the sick and the sinners. After his death and Resurrection, even more people became followers. Our Lord and Savior has haunted and challenged people for two thousand years to look him in the face and answer his call.

## Good Friday

The Church teaches us that Jesus redeemed and saved us when he died on the Cross for us. That is why we call the anniversary of his death "Good Friday". It certainly is an unusual use of language, as the usual custom is to celebrate births rather than deaths, and the death by execution of a good young man is usually seen as more of a disaster than as something to be celebrated.

We use the explanations of Jesus' death given in the New Testament, especially in the four Gospels and Saint Paul's letters (which adapt and develop Jewish theories of redemption or atonement from the sacrificial offering of animals). But the idea of redemption is common to many religions, based on the wish to be delivered from suffering, death and sin. The redemption is a mystery of faith, which reveals the hidden message of our Lord's life and death. While it does not go against reason, it requires a consent different from the logic required for agreeing that two plus two equals four. It is more like a historical explanation of God's activity.

Saint Paul explained it in a number of ways: "Christ died for our sins in accordance with the Scriptures" (1 Corinthians 15:3). Elsewhere, he wrote that "God was in Christ reconciling the world to himself" (2 Corinthians 5:19). He described Jesus, taking up a line of thought from the Old Testament prophet Isaiah, as the suffering servant who will "make many righteous; and he shall bear their iniquities" (Isaiah 53:11; Romans 5:19).

John, in his Gospel, described Christ as "the Lamb of God, who takes away the sins of the world" (John 1:29). His description was based on the Old Testament's image of the spotless lambs who were sacrificed to God at Passover time, in gratitude for the liberation of the Jewish people from Egypt under Moses' leadership.

Our Lord himself at the Last Supper on Holy Thursday, the night before he died, celebrated the first Mass, or Eucharist, as a memorial of his own sacrifice. "This is my body, which is given for you." "This is my blood of the covenant, which is poured out for many for the forgiveness of sins" (Luke 22:19–20; see also Matthew 26:26–28).

Through his redeeming death and Resurrection, Jesus ensured that God forgives us our sins and that good people are able to go to heaven, where they will find an eternity of reward and happiness. Jesus broke the hold of original sin on us.

It is no wonder that the Cross has become the best-known symbol of Christianity. Because of the Cross, people know that the Son of God understands their predicament; he has undergone suffering. In their faith in the Cross, people glimpse the truth that God can bring some supernatural good out of even the worst suffering.


## The Resurrection

In many countries more people go to church to celebrate Christmas than go for Good Friday or Easter Sunday (when we celebrate the fact that Jesus rose on the third day after his death). This seems to be more than a coincidence. Less faith is needed to celebrate a birth than a death, especially the birth and death of the Son of God. In countries with traditional Catholic cultures (such as Italy and Spain), Easter is a far bigger feast because the importance of the Resurrection has entered more truly into the public consciousness.

Many people today are also insensitive to the "last things", namely, death and judgment, heaven and hell. They avoid these issues. Some people spend more time planning their retirement than preparing for their death, when they will be judged by their Maker. This contrasts strongly with the New Testament times, when some believed that our Lord would return at any moment. Saint Paul had to insist that the Thessalonians continue at their tasks because they had decided to stop work, believing that Jesus would return in glory very soon.

The Resurrection is the crowning truth of the Christian faith. So crucial is this miracle that Saint Paul wrote that "If Christ has not been raised, then our preaching is in vain and your faith is in vain" (1 Corinthians 15:14). The Resurrection of Christ, body and soul, from the dead was a real event, attested to in all four Gospels. The empty tomb was an essential sign that first prompted the demoralized disciples to investigate whether the "impossible" had happened. The women were the first to encounter the risen Christ and inform the apostles, the primary witnesses of the Resurrection. Many others also saw Jesus; Saint Paul even spoke of five hundred witnesses at one time (1 Corinthians 15:4–8).

Although Thomas was able to place his hands in Jesus' wounds (John 20:27–29), the Resurrection was not a return to earthly life. After the Resurrection, Jesus' life was a glorified one beyond space and time, a confirmation of his divinity.

It is also taught by Christians that Christ will return on the last day to judge all people and separate the good from the evil, the wheat from the tares (Matthew 13:24–30). Then the conduct of each of us, our secret thoughts, will be brought to light (Mark 12:38–40). In the famous twenty-fifth chapter of Matthew's Gospel on this Last Judgment, it is stated that our attitude to our neighbors reveals our attitude to God: "As you did it to one of the least of my brethren, you did it to me" (Matthew 25:40). This is not poetry or metaphor but an article of faith; a truth Christ and the Church call us to believe. After death, Jesus still brings us life and light and truth.

*Bibliography*

*Catechism of the Catholic Church*, pt. 1, sec. 2, chap. 2, pars. 422–682.

● ● ● ● ● ● ● ● ● ● ● ● ● ● ● ● ● ● ● ● ● ● ● ●

*For Review*

1. For Christians Good Friday and Easter Sunday have a richer and deeper significance than a spring festival that celebrates birth and new growth. Explain why this is so.

2. What does redemption mean?

3. Why do we need to hear the message of Jesus today?

● ● ● ● ● ● ● ● ● ● ● ● ● ● ● ● ● ● ● ● ● ● ● ●

*Consider These*

1. Where have you found the most powerful description of Christ? In the Gospels; or a sermon; or some book? Describe the image and explain what made it so moving.

2. a. Is it inaccurate to describe our country as a post-Christian society? Why?

   b. Does the present situation make it more or less difficult for people who have deep Christian beliefs?

   c. Why do you think people need religion? What substitutes for religious belief has our society made? What other gods do people believe in?

3. How can Catholics best spread the message of Jesus Christ being the way, the truth and the life? Do you feel this obligation?

4. a. Do you accept Christ's teaching on suffering?

   b. Does faith make a difference in times of suffering?

*Extension Exercises*

1. One of the most popular pieces of music played to honor Christ is the "Alleluia Chorus" from George Frederick Handel's (1685–1759) oratorio *The Messiah*. This piece is still performed regularly, often at Christmas and Easter. What does this music express for you? Is *Pie Jesu* by the contemporary English composer Andrew Lloyd Weber better suited to today's tastes?

2. Napoleon (1769–1821), emperor of France and conqueror of Europe, said: "Alexander, Caesar, Charlemagne and I myself have founded empires; but upon what do these creations of our genius depend? Upon force! Jesus alone founded his empire upon love, and to this very day millions die for him." What is the secret of Jesus' continuing influence?

3. "He who understands Christ's teaching feels like a bird that did not know it had wings and now suddenly realizes that it can fly, can be free and no longer needs to fear"—Russian author Leo Tolstoy (1828–1910). Have you ever felt like this? How could Christ's teaching work in this way?

4. In his *A Letter to John Dryden*, James McAuley (1917–1976) wrote:

   > But if men ask where full peace lies indeed
   > You knew the answer, John, to strife of creed:
   > Christ is what men have in common, he,
   > He is the Word, the source of unity,
   > The Reason of man's reason, and its Light;
   > Those who participate in him, unite,
   > And those who turn their backs face
   > out to endless night.

a. What do you think is the speaker's attitude to Jesus?

b. Does this poem express your faith, your view of Christ?

c. What hymn or poem best expresses your approach to Christ our Lord?

# CHAPTER THREE

# What's God Like?

## *How do you see God?*

Jesus guides us to his Father. Jesus, we are taught, is the second Person of the Blessed Trinity. But who or what is God, and how can we know him? What will he mean for each one of us?

### The Design of the Universe

The universe is breathtaking in its complexity, enormity and beauty. It is awesome. Our sun belongs to the Milky Way galaxy with 100,000 million other stars. There are at least 100 million galaxies like ours. In fact, there are more stars in the universe than grains of sand on all the beaches of the world. Mathematicians have developed a shorthand way of expressing these huge numbers, for example, 100,000 million is represented by $10^{11}$.

There seem to be two possible ways in which the universe came to exist: by chance or by design. In the early 1980s, Chandra Wickramasinghe (an astrophysicist in Wales) and Fred Hoyle (a well-known British astronomer) decided to calculate the odds on whether random shuffling of amino acids could have produced life. They found that the odds were one chance in $10^{40,000}$ (an almost unimaginable number). Both these scientists had been atheists, but they came to believe through their scientific work that a creator exists.

The number of subatomic particles in the entire universe has been calculated at $10^{81}$. To claim that life came about by chance is like claiming that a runaway truck moving through a garbage dump could produce the Mona Lisa! Throughout history, most people have seen the mind of God in the design of the universe.

### God's Divine Nature

Saint Augustine of Hippo (354–430) wrote that God is "the light of our minds, the strength of our wills, the source of our joy". God is the eternal mystery of love.

The Church teaches that the one true God is merciful, all-powerful and ever faithful, the Creator of heaven and earth. God is good and wise, neither cruel nor capricious. God is infinite, without beginning and without end, the all-powerful Lord of history, who will oversee the final separation of the good from the bad.

Christians believe that God is a trinity of persons: God the Father, the source of all that is; the Son of God, i.e., Jesus Christ, true God and true man, who showed us by his life and teaching what God is like; and the Holy Spirit, who lives in the hearts of all the faithful.

There is no completely adequate explanation for this mystery of love, although many have tried to explain it. We are told that Saint Patrick likened the Trinity to the three leaves of a shamrock; others have used the three states of water (i.e., liquid, ice and steam); still others have compared the Trinity to a family or community or to a triangle overlaying a circle. What is most important, however, is to remember that God loves every one of us and keeps each of us in the palm of his hand. God is love and "everyone who loves is born of God and knows God" (1 John 4:7).

### Jesus' Picture of the Good God

Jesus was a remarkable teacher. His influence has endured and been more extensive than that of anyone else, even though he left no writings. To explain his basic doctrines, he used short stories, or parables. Jesus told the following parable, which explains the goodness of God (Luke 15:11–32).

There was a wild younger son who pestered his father for his share of the inheritance, obtained it and then left for the bright lights where he proceeded to spend his savings on riotous living. A recession hit, and in the absence of any social service benefits, the young fellow had to take a job looking after pigs. His situation represents the ultimate degradation. (The Talmud, the Jewish book of laws, says, "Cursed be the man who breeds swine.") The young man realized that he would be better off working at home and that he had wronged his father and sinned against heaven. He decided to travel home and try for a job on the family farm.

His father might have responded in a number of ways: for example, he might have explained to his son that there was no longer a place for him in the family or that the young man's mother had died as a result of his departure; or he might have wished his son well and offered him a job on an outlying part of the farm but explained that things had changed too much for his son to return to the family circle.

The father did none of these things. Rather, he ran to the young man, kissed him and gave him a fine robe and a beautiful ring as symbols of honor and authority. The father gave his son sandals so that he would not be barefoot like a slave. Meat was eaten rarely, but the father ordered the slaughter of the best fatted calf and a huge welcome-home party.

When the older brother returned home from work, he found the party in full swing. He complained bitterly to his father that his brother did not deserve such treatment and that he had never received such a reward despite his dutiful and loving behavior. In answer, the father explained to his older son that he was much appreciated and that the remainder of the inheritance was his, "but it was only right we should celebrate and rejoice, because your brother here was dead and has come to life, he was lost and is found" (Luke 15:32).

Every serious Christian who is conscious of personal weakness should be encouraged by this picture of the one good God in action.

## God as Spirit

What does it mean to describe God as a spirit? How important are the things of the spirit? Is the spiritual world real or imaginary? These questions are all hard to answer. Many people have difficulties trying to conceptualize God as a spirit. Indeed, some seem to see a spiritual God primarily as a social device like Santa Claus: socially useful for youngsters but not an object of adult belief. But the spirit of God is akin to parental love. It is real, powerful and invisible. Indeed, God is love itself.

When explained in these terms, it is easier to form an understanding of the spiritual. Gravity, magnetic forces, radio and television waves are also examples of real, powerful and invisible forces, which may offer points of comparison for understanding the spiritual.

Talking of the spirit gives us some idea of the problems in speaking about God because our human words do not fit God exactly. God is so different. When we say that God is loving and merciful, we realize that he is enormously more loving and merciful than the best human being. Sometimes, the terms we use about God are negative. For example, just as we start to explain the word "spiritual" by saying it is not material or physical, so infinite means "cannot be measured" and omnipotent means "no limits to God's powers".

Human reason can take us some considerable distance toward God, but God's revelations of himself through his Son have given us many more useful insights into the reality and workings of the mystery that lies behind the veil of physical reality.

## The Problem of Suffering

If God is all-loving and all-powerful, why do bad and terrible things happen, sometimes to good people? This is the biggest problem for believers, and no explanation is completely satisfactory, especially for those who experience great tragedies. Jesus' life shows God's suffering. Heaven is where unjust and disproportionate suffering is redressed; this is part of what Jesus meant when he said, "Blessed are those who mourn, they shall be comforted" (Matthew 5:4).

In the Old Testament times, the Jews were uncertain and divided on whether man survived after death. As practical people who believed in God, they concluded that the good were blessed with prosperity and that misfortune came from personal sins or the sins of ancestors. The Old Testament Book of Job wrestled with the problem of the sufferings of the just, and our Lord explicitly denied that misfortune is always linked to personal sins (Luke 13:1–5).

Disasters are either natural or created by men. Natural disasters, for example, droughts, floods, earthquakes and cyclones, sometimes cause great suffering. Most of these are completely beyond our control, but the sufferings they produce used to lead people to believe that God (or the gods) was cruel and capricious. Like us, they believed that God is the Creator and master of all nature. Similarly, they wondered how a good God could allow so much suffering. The key to this dilemma is to understand that nature, following its blind, relentless, mechanical laws, is different from a loving, forgiving God. God must be more than nature. As the old saying goes: God always forgives, man sometimes forgives, nature never forgives.

There is a fault-line that runs through all creation (and our hearts) back to Adam and Eve, our first parents. While human nature is basically good, we are also born selfish and have an inclination toward evil. We must curb and restrain our faults by following good examples, accepting support and by being loved. Christians call this "fault-line" original sin. In his wisdom, God has allowed human life to be a time of trial, a testing-ground for heaven.

No century in history has produced such human cruelty as the twentieth century. We have seen the First World War (1914–1918), during which four million people were killed in battle, the Second World War (1939–1945), which caused fifty million deaths, the genocide in Cambodia under Pol Pot (1976–1979), with at least one million killed, and the "ethnic cleansing" in Serbia, Bosnia and Croatia in the 1990s.

Modern science and technology, while providing much that is good, have increased enormously the human capacity for harm. The worst of human evil is a great mystery, far beyond the day-to-day weakness of most of us. God has given us the moral freedom to choose and the capacity to distinguish between good and evil. These abilities plus our high intelligence differentiate us from animals. They can be used for heroism and self-sacrifice or to inflict the most barbaric cruelties.

God does not usually intervene directly to combat evil, relying on us to do so—he must often be disappointed in us. A holy Jewish woman who died in the concentration camp at Auschwitz during the Second World War put it beautifully: "Poor God, so powerless".

Christians believe that they are saved (or redeemed) by the death of Jesus Christ, true God and true man, on the Cross. In other words, Christians believe that the most terrible and pointless suffering can be transformed by God, like the conversion of physical mass into energy, so suffering can produce blessings through the powerful reaction with grace and goodness.

We need faith to accept the redemptive dimension of suffering, as it is far beyond common sense. It is the most unusual of Christian beliefs: believing God will forgive the most terrible crimes if the sinner repents. However, atheists have a bigger problem than believers. The logical conclusion of atheism is that life has no purpose or meaning. As the French writer André Malraux challenged provocatively: "No atheist can explain the smile of a child." If there is no God, how do we explain so much goodness and beauty around us?

### The God of Love and Eternal Punishment

We have seen the welcome given to the returning prodigal son. Jesus urged the shepherd to leave the ninety-nine safe sheep to find the single wanderer. From his own words, we know that our Lord came among us to save rather than to condemn (John 3:17). Nonetheless, the Church also follows Jesus' teachings of the existence of hell: a place of punishment for the wicked (Matthew 13:42; John 5:28–29).

God never rejects any small gesture of friendship or repentance. No person goes to hell from weakness alone. Active malice is required. However, adults endowed with a free will can persist in refusing the spirit of love. Hell might be our choice, but it is not God's desire.

The concept of hell is a problem for many people today. Perhaps we should approach it from the point of view of the innocent victims of history's terrible crimes. Who are we to deny to the millions of victims of Hitler and Stalin and Pol Pot that their persecutors should be punished, perhaps for eternity, if they refuse to repent? Even if they did repent, God would require them to expiate their crimes before entry into the happiness of heaven. Justice is often incomplete in this life. God must balance up the scales in eternity.

## Doubts

Few young people who have the Christian message explained to them are unable to believe. However, doubts and difficulties are not uncommon. Genuine personal difficulties are never sinful, and life can throw up tragedies that test our faith in a God who is interested in us.

Our Lord told us that the pure in heart shall see God (Matthew 5:8) and the selfish love of evil (for example, greed, hate or promiscuity) will make it harder to believe or easier to lose our faith. Those who are confused and uncertain but want to believe should pray each day: "Dear God of love, if you exist, bring me to the truth." They should also make a special effort (and regularly) to help others, for example, through charitable organizations such as the Saint Vincent de Paul Society. They are likely to find God in the persons they serve.

*Bibliography*

*Catechism of the Catholic Church*, especially pt. 1, sec. 2, chap. 1, article 1, pars. 185–324.

See the article in *Time,* January 18, 1982, for more information on the scientists Wickramasinghe and Hoyle, discussed on page 23.

• • • • • • • • • • • • • • • • • • • • • • • •

*For Review*

1. Does the beauty/complexity and stability of life require a creator?

2. Why is there evil if God is loving and all-powerful?

3. What can we know about God?

• • • • • • • • • • • • • • • • • • • • • • • •

*Consider These*

1. How can the beauty of our world lead us to ideas about God?

2. a. Ask people who are believers for their ideas of God.

   b. What would you say to a person who says: "There can't be a God because there is so much evil around"?

   c. Is it easy or difficult to believe that there is a God? What are some ways of helping oneself when faith itself is a problem?

3. Is faith in Christ as the Son of God more difficult than faith in God?

4. Saint Augustine of Hippo (354–430) lost what little faith he had as a teenager and found the truth only as an adult. He said: "Our entire task in this life consists in healing the eyes of our heart so they may be able to see God" (Sermon 88.6). What is he talking about?

5. List some of the situations and activities that might prevent us or hinder us from believing in God.

*Extension Exercises*

1. Astronaut John Glenn said: "Galaxies, millions of light years across, all traveling in prescribed orbits in relation to one another! Could all this have just happened? Was this an accident that someone tossed up a bunch of flotsam and jetsam, and it suddenly started making these orbits of its own accord? I can't believe that's really true. I think this was a definite plan. This is one thing in space that shows me there is a God, some Power that put all this into orbit and keeps it there. It wasn't just an accident." Do you agree?

2. The Anglo-American poet T. S. Eliot (1888–1965) wrote the following poem:

> O Light Invisible, we praise Thee!
> Too bright for mortal vision.
> O Greater Light, we praise Thee for less:
> We thank Thee for the lights that we have kindled,
> The light of altar and of sanctuary:
> Small lights of those who meditate at midnight
> And lights directed through the coloured panes of windows
> And light reflected from the polished stone,
> The gilded carven wood, the coloured fresco.
> Our gaze is submarine, our eyes look upward
> And see the light that fractures through unquiet water.
> We see the light but see not whence it comes,
> O Light Invisible, we glorify Thee!

Does Eliot's poem help you to pray or think of God?

3. The following quotation is from Thomas Merton's *No Man Is an Island.*

> If we strive to be happy by filling all the silences of life with sound, productive by turning all our being into doing, we will only succeed in producing a hell on earth.

> If we have no silence, God is not heard in our
> music. If we have no rest, God does not bless our
> work. If we twist our lives out of shape in order to fill
> every corner of them with action and experience,
> God will silently withdraw from our hearts and leave
> us empty.

Do you agree with Merton? Is silence necessary, even for our health?

4. To choose a piece of music that comes closest to expressing something of God's greatness, transcendence and mystery is an enormously difficult task. One suggestion is the setting of the "Miserere" psalm by the Italian composer Gregory Allegri (1582–1652), sung each year in the Sistine Chapel at the Vatican during Holy Week. This composition was kept a papal secret until 1840, although Mozart copied it from memory after hearing it when he was only fourteen—an extraordinary feat! Another beautiful piece is the Adagio in G Minor attributed to the Italian composer Thomas Albinoni (1671–1751). Albert Einstein (1879–1955) was the most famous scientist of the twentieth century. He loved music, although he was himself an indifferent musician. After listening to a particularly beautiful recital, he embraced the artist and said: "Now I know that there is a God."

a. Do you ever feel like this? Do you ever experience religious awe while listening to music?

b. What sort of music makes you feel closest to God?

# CHAPTER FOUR

# Why Go to Mass?

*How do you worship God?*

"Mass is boring!" is a common expression among many young Catholics. Yet the Church takes its importance so seriously that she insists that we attend Mass once a week. What is so special about Mass?

### Mass Obligation

Jesus told us that God loves every one of us better than any parent because he is our loving Father. We need to acknowledge this, to thank God for what we have, to praise him, to ask his forgiveness for our sins and to pray for what we need—not once in a while, but regularly.

Therefore, the Church teaches that we all have a serious obligation to worship the one true God each Sunday in the celebration of the Eucharist. If we rarely (or never) visited our parents when this could be done, we would know we were doing the wrong thing. Is our duty to God any less?

Going to Mass on Sunday is as old as Christianity itself. By doing so, we demonstrate our loyalty to Christ and his Church and our hope for salvation in the next life, and we show that the Catholic community (locally and throughout the world) is united in faith and charity.

## The Eucharist Is Central

What is special about the Mass? What is supposed to happen? Some people feel they can pray better out in the forest or down at the beach. Although people pray at different times and in different circumstances, Christ recommended the ritual and prayers of the Eucharist when he urged us to "Do this as a memorial of me" (Luke 22:19).

Saint Paul's letter to the Christians of Corinth is among the earliest writings in the New Testament, written from Ephesus in about A.D. 55. In it, Paul tells us of the Eucharist: "For this is what I received from the Lord, and in turn passed on to you: that on the same night that he was betrayed, the Lord Jesus took some bread, and thanked God for it and broke it, and he said 'This is my body, which is for you; do this as a memorial of me.' In the same way he took the cup after supper, and said 'This cup is the new covenant in my blood. Whenever you drink it, do this as a memorial of me.' Until the Lord comes, therefore, every time you eat this bread and drink this cup, you are proclaiming his death" (1 Corinthians 11:23–26). In other words, the Eucharist links the Church to Christ's sacrificial offering of himself to God, and the fruits of his life, death and Resurrection are made available to us. We receive spiritual strength, which the Church calls grace, from this action.

Only an ordained priest can say Mass. Acting through the power of the Holy Spirit and representing Christ, the priest consecrates the bread and wine so that they become really and truly the body and blood of Christ.

When Christ was preaching in Palestine, he promised his followers that he would give them his flesh to eat and his blood to drink and that "anyone who eats this bread will live forever" (John 6:58). Some thought such language was intolerable and "after this, many of his disciples left him and stopped going with him" (John 6:66). Even today, many people, including some Christians, find it impossible to accept that the bread and wine are not just symbols but truly the body and blood of Christ. But this is what true Catholics believe.

## Sundays Are Special

Christians believe that Sunday is a holy day as well as a holiday. It is the day of the Lord, which sets it apart from the rest of the week. Weekends should be family times for being together, for rest and recreation, and part of Sunday should belong explicitly to God. This time also reminds us that there is more to life than making money and working. One hour a week for our Creator, the one great God, is no big deal.

The Christian Sunday is a development of the Jewish Sabbath, which is celebrated each Saturday. In the story of creation recounted in the Old Testament Book of Genesis, we are told that God rested on the seventh day. Therefore, a regular feature of Jewish life has always been the Sabbath, which is devoted to prayer and rest. On this day, Jewish people also remember how God used Moses to lead the Jews on the exodus from Egypt into the freedom of the Promised Land. This event is of immense national and religious significance because the Jews are not just another group of people loved by God, but his chosen people, a people with whom God made a unique alliance, to whom he revealed himself and who became (and remain) special agents in salvation history. All this is remembered each Sabbath. For Jews, the day begins at dusk on the previous evening, rather than at midnight, which explains how Saturday night Mass fulfills our Sunday obligation.

Jesus and his followers were sometimes accused of not respecting the law that forbade work on the day of rest, for example, when Jesus cured sick people on the Sabbath (Mark 3:5) and the disciples picked a few ears of corn while walking through the cornfield (Mark 2:24). With typical skill and common sense, our Lord rejected this carping criticism, and while recognizing the importance and holiness of the Sabbath day (see, for example, Mark 1:21), he pointed out that "the Sabbath was made for man, not man for the Sabbath, so the Son of Man is master even of the Sabbath" (Mark 2:27).

Through his death and Resurrection, Jesus redeemed us. We could say he started a new religion, or at least a new stage of religion, because after his time on earth, there was a new arrangement formed between God and his chosen followers: the old law was replaced by the new law of love. Jesus completed the work of redemption by rising from the dead on the first day of the week (Matthew 28:1; Luke 24:1), and so it is not surprising that for the first Christian communities, Sunday became the day of the Lord, when they commemorated Christ's new creation in their eucharistic celebrations.

## Praying at Mass

No one can truly join in the Eucharist without faith. If a person is unable or refuses to believe in God, then he will probably feel unable to pray. The Mass is basically a form of prayer. In fact, for Catholics, the Eucharist is far and away the most important prayer, when a group of people, around the priest, come to praise God. Therefore, faith is essential for participation in the Mass.

Some people come to Mass looking for a good performance, just as we seek a classy concert or a close football game. But a friendly atmosphere, great music and an interesting sermon are only truly effective if they are prayerful and help us to pray.

The vestments, the ritual actions of the priest, and the set prayers and hymns are all designed to open our hearts and minds to the mystery of God. This is not cheap magic nor fast-moving entertainment, but symbolism that helps to carry us toward the transcendent.

Those who are genuinely unable to believe yet who want to know the truth should pray, asking God to bring them to the truth. They should do this every day. Doubts and difficulties with faith are nothing new and not even unknown among the faithful. Saint Thomas the Apostle refused to believe Jesus had risen until he placed his hand in our Lord's side. Only then did he acknowledge in faith, "My Lord and my God" (John 20:24–28).

## Bored at Mass?

While it is true that one cannot understand the Eucharist without faith, it is also, alas, true that many young Catholic people are often bored at Mass. But people can be bored for a variety of reasons, and many different categories of people attend Mass. We are usually bored by what we do not understand, whether it is a difficult chemistry lesson or a type of music or sport with which we are unacquainted. Moreover, the faithful at Mass are supposed to be more than spectators—we all have to make an effort. Mass is for the worship of God; it is not supposed to be like going to the gym or to the movies.

Some young people go to Mass mainly to please their parents, while others choose to stay away because they do not like to be told what they should be doing by the Church or by their parents. Some people, young and old, do not have the courage to stand out against the crowd and go to Mass regularly, while others claim they "get nothing out of it" when they go.

Although such people often know something about prayer and are keen to know more about God, they need to find a way around the problem of not wanting to attend Mass. Where minds are hostile or closed, then a mood change is necessary in order to discover how Mass can become more interesting and life-giving. Nevertheless, we should not claim that every Mass will be pleasant and enjoyable.

## Catholic Hostility

Some Catholic teenagers are derisive when their friends go to Mass. This means that students from church-going Catholic families need to be firm in classroom discussions and elsewhere in order to explain, without apology, why they are regular worshippers.

Reasons for the scoffing or ribbing often vary. Some people enjoy a bit of argument and discussion, while others like to see whether churchgoers are people of habit or conviction. A few may feel guilty about not going themselves and find the regular worship by their peers a silent rebuke. Others might be irritated by some strict Church teachings and so vent their hostility through criticism.

Such peer-group pressures are not common; nevertheless, they do exist in some Catholic schools. However, strong Catholic influences (and a minority is powerful enough to achieve strength) will neutralize these hostile attitudes.

## Unity and Tradition

The basic elements of the Catholic Eucharist are the same everywhere and remain as they have been throughout the Church's two-thousand-year history. The prayers and symbolism of the ritual remain faithful to the gospel teaching and unite us with the universal Church and tap into the collective memory of our worshipping ancestors.

There is considerable variety allowed in the different readings, hymns and music and vast differences of style in ceremonies (for example, the Easter Vigil celebrated in a cathedral or a small home Mass). But the strict liturgical guidelines of the Church are there to ensure the fundamental worldwide unity of faith and worship. The celebration should be regarded as an act of worship, and not as group therapy or entertainment.

After we gather together for prayer, often confessing our sins in preparation for the sacred moments to follow, we have the Liturgy of the Word, i.e., readings from the Old and New Testaments and from the Gospels. On Sundays and feast days the priest will give a homily or teaching. After this comes the Liturgy of the Eucharist itself, with the offering of the bread and wine, their consecration into the body and blood of Christ as the priest recites Christ's words, the remembering of Christ's redeeming activity, the intercessions, the breaking of the bread and the distribution of communion. All this is essential.

Prayer should not always be hard work, but sometimes it is difficult. Christians persevere with prayer, not because it is always easy or interesting, but because it is intrinsically worthwhile.

**Sign of Unity**

We all remember our first communion, received after an intensive preparation so that we would better understand what we were doing. When we visit friends and are offered food and drink, it is good manners to accept this hospitality and considered rude to refuse for no good reason. Going to communion is not like this. We are not eating bread and drinking wine together as a sign of friendship but receiving the body and blood of the Lord.

Only Catholics may receive communion at a Catholic Mass. Taking communion is a sign that we belong to the Catholic Church and is reserved for members only. This is not snobbishness but an undertaking to preserve respect for the ritual and honesty. Church membership is more than a formality.

However, Catholics who are aware that they are in a state of very serious (mortal or death-bearing) sin should not go to communion before repenting and going to the sacrament of reconciliation. This teaching comes from Saint Paul himself and is a constant Catholic tradition: "Everyone is to recollect himself before eating this bread and drinking this cup; because a person who eats and drinks without recognizing the Body is eating and drinking his own condemnation" (1 Corinthians 11:28–29).

Catholics in good standing are encouraged to go to communion at their regular Masses (once a year is a minimum requirement). However, it is incongruous for Catholics who rarely go to Mass to receive communion (for example, at weddings or school Masses) unless they have been to reconciliation beforehand. Our grandparents were told that "It is the Mass that matters." This will always be true.

* * * * * * * * * * * * * * * * * * * * * * * * *

## Bibliography

*Catechism of the Catholic Church*, pt. 2, sec. 1, chaps. 1–2, pars. 1076–1209; pt. 2, sec. 2, chap. 1, art. 3, pars. 1322–1419; pt. 3, sec. 2, chap. 1, art. 3, pars. 2168–95.

*For Review*

1. What do the priest and people celebrate and remember in the Mass?

2. Explain how Sunday came to be an important day in Church life.

3. Why does Mass always follow the same pattern?

*Consider These*

1. How do you feel about attending Mass? What are the differences between the Masses that you attend in different churches?

2. What is more important at Mass: the externals or the hidden mystery? What is commemorated?

3. How does Sunday Mass attendance enrich the community life of the Church?

4. Why are the Mass readings always from the Scriptures?

5. How do you pray during Mass?

6. Can you "get something" out of Mass, even if you don't enjoy it?

*Extension Exercises*

1. Many great composers have set the Mass to music. One famous composition is the majestic Mass in B Minor by Johann Sebas-

tian Bach (1685–1750), who was a Lutheran. Gregorian chant provides other great settings for the Mass. Among these is the Canto Gregoriano, recorded on a CD titled *Chant* by the Spanish Benedictine monks of the monastery of Santo Domingo de Silas. Ask your teacher or the school music teacher to select and play excerpts from a selection of pieces written for the Mass. Discuss the mood and tone of the music. What impact does it have on the listener?

2. The great cathedrals of the world provide different architectural settings for the celebration of the Eucharist. How is Saint Peter's cathedral in Rome different from the great Gothic cathedrals? How are the beautiful Orthodox cathedrals different again?

# CHAPTER FIVE

# Families: Do We Need Them?

*What is good about families?*

Going to Mass is a way of uniting with God's family. We also have our own personal families with whom we connect. What is the family, and why does the Church insist on its importance in our lives?

## What Is the Family?

God designed human nature so that men and women would complement each other and so that the human race would continue. Therefore, the family too is a natural unit, made up of a man and woman, united in marriage, with their children. Sometimes, death and marriage breakups complicate the situation, but a married couple with children remains the norm and the ideal. Extended families, grandparents, aunts, uncles and cousins are usually sources of much happiness and support. It is unfortunate that today's life-style often discourages people from maintaining extended family links. The Catholic Church encourages these wider loyalties because they bring many practical advantages, such as the availability of help or friendship in times of trouble or loneliness.

### Changing Families in the United States

The basic institution of the family is at the heart of all social life. However, within that pattern, there are wide variations and there have been significant changes.

Because people are generally living to a greater age, marriages now last four times longer than they did last century. In Australia in 1911, the average marriage lasted twenty-eight years; in 1967, forty-two years was the average. Soon, fifty years may be the possible average (barring divorce or death). But unfortunately, marriage breakdowns have increased. In the United States in 1960, only 25 percent of all marriages ended in divorce, but in 1986, 49 percent of marriages did. 13.9 percent of all people in the United States age 18 and older had been divorced in 1988, as opposed to only 4.3 percent in 1970. Consequently, there were many more single-parent families than there were previously.

The birth rate has dropped throughout the Western world. In the United States in 1910, the average number of children born per each married woman was 4.38. In 1970, the average number was 3.58 and in 1988, the number was 3.17. In the 1920s, mothers had one chance in one hundred of dying in childbirth; now it is one in five thousand. Today, children are more likely to know their grandparents, and even their great grandparents, but there are few extended and multigenerational families living together. Though most children still live with both of their biological parents in a "nuclear family", many now have TVs and VCRs, video and computer games, internet and e-mail that occupy their time.

Because of these distractions and work patterns, fewer families sit down together at meal times.

There are other changes too. Couples are marrying later in life (on average, at twenty-seven years of age for men, and twenty-four years of age for women). Many mothers have paid employment outside the home. There is an increase in common law marriages, and the marriage rate has dropped from 9.1 for every thousand people in 1971 to 6.6 in 1992. There is a decrease in the number of couples that are having children. In the United States in 1970, 44 percent of married couples had no children. In 1988, 51 percent of married couples did not. An increasing minority (40 percent in New York state in 1987) do not get married in a church.

## Catholics and Marriage

Marriage and the family exist for the sake of the mutual enrichment of husband and wife and for the procreation and education of children. Unfortunately today, there are couples who decide never to have children. No person is an island and no generation is the center of the universe. Marriage exists for the next generation and must be open to the possibility of children. So seriously does the Church view this obligation that a consistent refusal to have children can be one ground for the annulment of a marriage by a Church court. A Church annulment, which is not the same as a civil divorce, means that an essential constituent of marriage was never present.

To be married by a Catholic priest, it is necessary to accept that marriage is a lifelong contract, "for richer or poorer, in sickness or in health, until death". Catholics should not get married to see "if things work out" or "on condition that things work out".

The public promises of a bride and groom to each other, made before God, priest, family and friends, represent a mutual decision and commitment to make the marriage work through difficult as well as enjoyable times. The vows also aim to provide enormous security and consolation to partners and later to children.

Saint Paul said that the love of husband and wife should be like the love of Christ for the Church (Ephesians 5:32) so that the unity and community in a family are like the communion of Father, Son and the Spirit within the Godhead. So Catholics are required to be married before a priest in a Church ceremony, explicitly to ask God's blessing on probably the most important decision in adult life.

### Families and Mutual Responsibility

Christ and the Church have always emphasized mutual responsibilities. The Church (and Jesus) built on the older Jewish traditions so that the Judaeo-Christian system of marriage and family goes back for well over three thousand years. It has stood the test of time and is still effective. The permissive society of recent times does not work: its recipes for drugs, alcohol, pornography and sexual irresponsibility have increased the sum of human misery. Christian families work—and work well.

We are told in the New Testament that Jesus was obedient to his parents: in Nazareth he "lived under their authority" (Luke 2:51). He later quoted the teaching of Moses (Exodus 20:12), who said that children must honor and do their duty to their father and mother (Mark 7:10). Saint Paul takes up the theme and points out that this commandment is the first to have a promise attached to it—that "you will prosper and have a long life in the land" (Ephesians 6:1–3).

Naturally, the duty of obedience changes as the child grows up and becomes independent, but the duty of love and respect remains forever, especially when parents become old and sick. Our society does not cope very well with images of sickness and death. People who are sick, old or dying are often removed from the community because there is generally little acceptance of those aspects of life. However, as Christians, we have to battle our fears and do our duty to our loved ones. We should not give in to the tendency to push suffering and death out of sight and out of mind.

Grown-up children, who may often have their own families, have an opportunity with their elderly parents to return the love and care they received as children. It is most unfortunate that so many elderly people are neglected by their families and are very lonely, even if they are well cared for in nursing homes.

46

Parents have solemn obligations to their children: to love and provide for them, to give good example, to teach them the faith and to exercise wise discipline. Saint Paul explains succinctly, "parents, never drive your children to resentment, but in bringing them up, correct them and guide them as the Lord does" (Ephesians 6:4). When young, we often do not realize how good our parents are to us. When things go wrong, we should not be too quick to judge our parents but should try to consider their motives and reasons for acting.

### Divorce and Remarriage

Why is the Catholic Church so opposed to divorce and remarriage? Isn't it far better that parents split up rather than for everyone to stay together, fighting and suffering? The Church always has sympathy for those caught up in marriage breakdowns. However, all three Synoptic Gospels (Matthew 5:31–32, 19:3–9; Mark 10:9; Luke 16:18) and Saint Paul in his first letter to the Corinthians (1 Corinthians 7:10–11) report our Lord's strict teaching on the indissolubility of marriage, which was the original plan of the Creator. When it was made, this law was stricter than much contemporary Jewish practice, but Jesus explained that Moses allowed men to divorce their wives only because of human hardness of heart, because they "were so unteachable" (Matthew 19:8). On hearing this, some of the disciples said to him, "If that is how things are between husband and wife, it is not advisable to marry." But he replied, "It is not everyone who can accept what I have said, but only those to whom it is granted" (Matthew 19:10–12). Certainly, this is tough teaching, but it appears that quick, easy and automatic divorces in which blame is not attached to either partner are making a difficult situation worse rather than better.

Even governments, which usually lag behind public opinion, are worried about the institution of the family and about the increase in divorce statistics, hence, the International Year of the Family in 1994. Why should the family be the only institution where public promises, in fact a contract, can be broken with impunity? Nevertheless, the Church does not require a partner to remain in a truly impossible situation, but in such cases allows separation (without remarriage while the partner is living).

In the past, many parents stayed together for the sake of the children. A survey conducted in the United Kingdom in 1958 concluded that predivorce feuding was the main cause of damage to children. This view is widespread today. However, the authors of a 1994 investigation entitled the *Exeter Family Study*, which focused on the children and not the parents of "intact" families, were shaken by the unhappiness of children from "reordered" families. Such children were more than twice as likely to think badly of themselves, to have problems with schoolwork, to be ill regularly and to describe themselves as miserable. Most of the time, losing a parent caused the damage. According to the *Exeter Family Study*, divorce is often a running sore, where the suffering reverberates for years, especially with the children. Interestingly, three-quarters of noncustodial parents also wish they had not divorced.

In Brazil there was a piece of graffiti scrawled on a train: "Those who petition for divorce use the ink of their children's tears." Are we going to find more and more defenders of our Lord's teaching against divorce and remarriage among the children of the divorced?

## Marriage in the Life of Jesus

Our Lord did not marry and seems to have said some harsh things about the family. Is that why Catholic priests are not permitted to marry? What does all this mean for Christian theories on the family?

Jesus was born into the Jewish religion and fully recognized the Jewish doctrines on the need for family love. However, some of his teachings were provocative, for example, "If any man comes to me without hating his father, mother, wife, children, brothers, sisters, yes and his own life too, he cannot be my disciple" (Luke 14:2–6).

Jesus used the Aramaic language for preaching. In that language, the word "hate" (as used in the quotation above) means "to reject" or "set to one side" rather than actively to feel ill will. Our

48

Lord was telling us what must come first and that we cannot serve two masters. God should always come first, and family love, however beautiful, is not the ultimate love. Natural loves can be rivals to the Christian ideal of universal love and the necessary service of God.

Jesus, like his mother Mary and Saint John the Baptist, remained a virgin. He esteemed virginity, especially for religious motives: "There are eunuchs who have made themselves that way for the sake of the kingdom of heaven. Let anyone accept this who can" (Matthew 19:12). Virginity lived in faith and service, not selfishness, is a sign of the higher spiritual values of God's kingdom.

Most Catholic priests in the West belong to the Latin rite (or family) of the Church and must not marry. The Church asks them to follow the example of Christ and sacrifice the option of marriage and family for the sake of God's kingdom, especially through their service of people, inside and outside the Church, as ministerial priests. There are also many nuns and religious brothers, as well as lay women and men, who live celibate lives for God and the Church. However, there are other rites or families within the one Church that are fully Catholic but do not require all their priests to be unmarried, for example, the Ukrainian, Chaldean and Maronite rites.

Latin rite priests recognize that in following Christ's example of virginity, they are giving up something that is good and holy, namely, marriage. Priests defend marriage and family and enjoy being part of their larger family circle.

## Religion and Families

Statistics on family life show the good consequences of regular prayer, practical love and forgiveness, moral standards, the ideal of service, the importance of keeping promises and of struggling to live out the gospel teaching that the grain of wheat must die to produce a rich harvest (John 12:24).

While 49 percent of all marriages end in divorce in the United States, less that 5 percent of couples divorce who are following the Church's teaching on birth control. These couples use Natural

Family Planning when they need to limit the size of their families rather than using artificial contraception. It is interesting that those who live together before marriage are twice as likely to divorce as those who do not.

There is no automatic or magical connection between religious commitment and good marriages and families, but there is an important correlation. In the 1950s, a priest popularized the saying that the family that prays together stays together. There seems to be more in his message than meets the eye!

• • • • • • • • • • • • • • • • • • • • • • • • •

## Bibliography

*Catechism of the Catholic Church*, especially 2196–2257.

The following sources were used to research the statistics quoted throughout this chapter:

*Almanac of the 50 States: Basic Data Profiles with Comparative Tables,* ed. Hornor, Edith R. (Palo Alto: Information Publications, 1990).

*Population of the United States: Trends and Prospects, 1950–1990* (Washington, D.C.: Bureau of the Census, 1974),  p. 17

*Statistical Abstract of the United States 1990*, (U.S. Bureau of the Census, Washington, D.C., 1990), pp. 43, 51, 86.

*Vital Statistics of the United States*, 1987, National Center for Health Statistics (Hyattsville, Md.: U.S. Department of Health and Human Services, 1991).

Browning, Don, "Rebuilding the Nest: Families and the Need for a New Social Agenda", 1994 Rerum Novarum Lecture, Melbourne.

Crockett, Monica, and John Tripp, *The Exeter Family Study: Family Breakdown and Its Impact on Children* (University of Exeter Press, 1994).

Glenn, Norval D., *The Re-evaluation of Family Change by American Social Scientists* (Australian Catholic University, June 1994).

Smith, Janet E., *Why Humanae Vitae Was Right: A Reader* (San Francisco: Ignatius Press, 1993).

*For Review*

1. Why do Catholics rate marriage and family so highly?

2. Explain why the Catholic Church is opposed to divorce and remarriage.

3. What place do children have in the Catholic scheme of things?

*Consider These*

1. Discuss how broken families affect the lives of children.

2. What can society do to help more families stay together?

3. How does each member of the family contribute to the welfare of the whole family? Can teenagers damage family life?

4. Families are a good thing. But when the Church reinforces family life in particular ways, such as through her restriction of sexual activity to marriage or by discouraging divorce, much of

society is often hostile. Can good marriages and happy families be maintained without sacrifices and difficult choices?

5. What do parents owe their children? What do children owe their parents?

6. What is meant by the term "welfare state"? Are current government policies and practices helping to weaken or strengthen families?

7. What are some good ways of establishing family prayer?

8. How successful are common law marriages? Do they make for fulfilling and enjoyable families? Do they protect children? Do they protect the partners?

• • • • • • • • • • • • • • • • • • • • • • • • •

## Extension Exercises

1. Investigate different portrayals of family life on television. What sorts of families are projected? Does the screening time slot make a difference? What major attitudes are presented?

2. The *Domestic Symphony*, written by the German composer Richard Strauss (1864–1949), charts the delights and trials of typical family life. What music best expresses your family's characteristics?

3. Someone said that in much of the best-known literature, the novelists write about unhappy families rather than about happy families. Is this true, do you think?

4. Bruce Dawe wrote the following poem, entitled "Husband and Wife":

> The old jokes aren't as funny as they were,
> Nor the old jokers
> —Trailing in from the sun on a hot day
> Almost have meaning in an unmeant way.

Disintegrates into an easy-chair, cries "Phew!"
As if he'd nearly missed a vital cue:
"I must be getting old or something, Ann!"
Who turns and puts an arm about this man
(Incipient baldness being one more tree
Notched on the bush-track to eternity)
And rubs her face against his, saying "You
And me both, brother!" and the rest
Is silence (as it should be).

This seems best,
To mark the sweet breath of the half-mown lawn,
Not knowing whether to rejoice or mourn,
Summer trimming the hedge with shears of light,
While both of them, respectful of the night,
Kiss in the indoor dusk, even as they do
Making each particular thing less true.

a. Write a paragraph to describe the relationship of the husband and wife portrayed in Bruce Dawe's poem.

b. What can young people do to prepare for a lifelong and happy marriage? Can the Church help? What forces work against good marriages?

# CHAPTER SIX

# Why Help the Poor?

*Why doesn't our society tolerate failure?*

Successful family living enables us to look beyond ourselves, to become unselfish and to assume social responsibilities. How can we act as God's agents in the world? Why should we do this?

**The Poor Are Always with Us**

Young people often ask, innocently enough, why should Christians help the poor, the suffering, the unfortunate, especially when they are unknown to us, perhaps even in distant lands?

Simon of Cyrene was the passer-by, traveling into Jerusalem from the country, who was pressed into helping Jesus carry his Cross to Calvary. There is no evidence that he volunteered for this. Minding his own business, not wanting to bring attention to himself or get into trouble, he was in the right place at the right time. His simple act of kindness and support toward a condemned victim turned out to be a great blessing because he was assisting the Son of God himself.

Each person is precious because everyone is made in the image of God. Christ told us that when we help someone—even the least important or the most ungrateful—it is as though we are helping Christ himself.

## Jesus' Attitude toward the Poor

Jesus was born in a stable, and although his foster-father, Joseph, was a carpenter, Jesus' family was not rich. He lived as a poor man, unconcerned with possessions.

The poor had a special place in his scheme of things. When John the Baptist was in prison, he sent his followers to ask whether Jesus was the Messiah, the religious leader they were seeking. Our Lord replied, "Go back and tell John what you have seen and heard: the blind see again, the lame walk, lepers are cleansed, and the deaf hear, the dead are raised to life, the Good News is proclaimed to the poor" (Luke 7:21–22).

These words are based on chapter 61 of the Old Testament prophet Isaiah, the text that our Lord used in his home-town synagogue at Nazareth to announce his public ministry in Galilee. So it is no coincidence that the first of the Beatitudes from the Sermon on the Mount begins like this: "How blessed are the poor in spirit; theirs in the kingdom of heaven" (Matthew 5:3). The Beatitudes spell out the values that will be important in the next life, the values of God's kingdom. They are very different from the values of the society in which we live.

Our Lord stated clearly (and unapologetically) that all his followers should help the poor. For him, the poor had a special place.

## Jesus' Attitude toward the Rich

Most of us do not think of ourselves as rich, although we are aware that many other nations are poorer than ours. Most of us think of material wealth as a blessing. Therefore, we are surprised and discomforted to find that Jesus condemned riches more often than he condemned hypocrisy.

Certainly the message is a clear one: "It is easier for a camel to pass through the eye of a needle than for a rich man to enter the kingdom of heaven" (Matthew 19:24). After Luke's list of Beatitudes, we have the woes or curses, which begin: "But alas for you who are rich, you are having your consolation now" (Luke 6:24).

The other New Testament writers take up Jesus' theme. For example, the epistle to Timothy warns the rich not to look down on others and not to set their hopes on money (1 Timothy 6:17), and the epistle of James has a furious denunciation of those rich people who are corrupt, uncaring and murderers (James 5:1–6).

How can we explain all this? As we stand under the word of God, we are not entitled to explain away difficult teachings, but we are obliged to try and work out their proper meaning.

Our Lord was not an exponent of class warfare. His message of universal love and salvation was offered to all, including the rich (see, for example, Luke 16:9; Matthew 19:25). He loved sinners and called them to repentance. He dined happily with Zacchaeus, the rich tax collector (Luke 19:1–10).

At that time in Palestine, there was a great gulf between the wealthy minority and the poor majority, although Jewish law did strive to limit oppression and protect the powerless. The group Jesus condemned was a small coterie of cruel, rich exploiters. He was not opposed to proper rewards for hard-working people. It was the Lord Jesus himself who said, "There is more happiness in giving than in receiving" (Acts 20:35).

## Rich Followers of Christ

In the Western world, we enjoy a way of life better than that enjoyed by 95 percent of all the people who have ever lived. We should thank God for this, but definite obligations follow from our status. The first is to admit that we are better off than most.

In his 1993 encyclical on moral matters entitled *Veritatis Splendor*, Pope John Paul II began with the story of the rich young man who asked our Lord, "Teacher, what good must I do to have eternal life?" He was told to keep the commandments, to which he replied that he was already doing so. Then came the ultimatum: "If you wish to be perfect, go, sell your possessions and give the money to the poor, and you will have treasure in heaven; then come, follow me" (Matthew 19:16–21). The young fellow, who was very rich, turned away sadly, unable to make such a sacrifice. But in every age, there have been men and women prepared to do so for Christ's sake. Some go even farther; for example, the Missionaries of Charity (founded by Mother Teresa in Calcutta) make vows of poverty and service to the poorest of the poor.

Our Lord realized that most of his followers would not have the strength to seek perfection in this radical way. Indeed, some of his own disciples were quite prosperous: probably Mary, Martha and Lazarus; certainly Joseph of Arimathaea, who provided the tomb for Jesus' burial.

Joseph realized that all true followers of God use some of their money to help the poor; those who have chosen Mammon and are slaves to money keep it all for themselves. True riches are to be found in what we give, not in what we possess. The real scandal in the story of Lazarus and the rich man in purple and fine linen who feasted every day lies not in the coexistence of rich and poor but in the fact that Lazarus did not receive even a crumb from the rich man's table (Luke 16:19–31).

In the Old Testament, prosperity is seen as a blessing for those who love God and a reward for fidelity; a long line of notables from Abraham to David were so blessed. Even Job recovers his prosperity after his terrible trials. Our Lord took a quite different tack: "Do not store up treasures for yourselves on earth . . . but store up treasures for yourselves in heaven" (Matthew 6:19–20). He was also quite clear that each person has to choose: "No one can be the slave of two masters. . . . You cannot be the slave both of God and of money" (Matthew 6:24).

When we are rich it is easy to forget that all good things come from God and that God is the master of life and death. Remember the rich farmer who was planning to lead the good life for many years and was called that very night to heaven (Luke 12:16–21)! Every possession and accomplishment comes at some cost, and modern life shows that intense attachments to money, possessions and pleasure make it harder to believe in God and in an afterlife of happiness. The decline of faith and religious practice, evident even in the Catholic community, is certainly connected with the rise of materialism (where money takes first place).

## Charity and Justice

Nobody can give what he does not possess, but helping the poor, who can be defined in many ways, is essential for followers of Christ. Our Lord could not have made this point more emphatically than in his description of the Last Judgment, when there will be the final separation of the good from the evil, the sheep from the goats, by the Son of Man. The good will proceed to the kingdom of eternal life and happiness, while the wicked will be condemned to the punishment of eternal fire. What separates the good from the bad?

Those rewarded with heaven are the people who fed Christ when he was hungry, gave him a drink when he was thirsty, visited him in jail, clothed him and made him welcome. They will exclaim that they cannot remember meeting Christ and the reply will come, "insofar as you did this to one of the least of these brothers of mine, you did it to me." The others are lost because they did not care, because they failed to recognize Christ in their needy brothers and sisters (Matthew 25:31–46).

The vast network of Catholic charitable organizations and all the Catholic activities for social justice are our attempt to practice what Christ preached, to see Christ in the poor and suffering. All of us must help in some way.

**Charity Begins at Home**

Our first obligation is to our own people, to our poor. Charity does begin at home, for instance with the unemployed. We need to work hard to ensure that poverty and family breakdown do not run together to produce a permanent underclass of people.

The Catholic Church contributes to government programs that aim to help the long-term unemployed. Nearly every Catholic parish has its Saint Vincent de Paul group, and some schools and parishes also have groups of young Vincentians to help the needy. The Saint Vincent de Paul groups throughout the world distribute help worth millions of dollars. Just as importantly, their visits often bring support and encouragement.

Yet, despite the conditions of poverty in our country, we are rich by the standards of many Third World countries. For example, in Thailand, which is one of the more prosperous countries in Asia, a production worker's hourly wage is only about 69 cents. In the Philippines the rate is 57 cents, while in Indonesia it is only about 39 cents. By these standards, we are certainly rich.

Most people who help the poor in our country will also help the needy overseas, while those who refuse to help overseas are often those who will do little or nothing for their fellow Americans. Many people would be surprised at how effective even small amounts of money can be when used properly.

Partly as a result of assistance offered by charitable organizations, significant progress has been made over the years in the standards of health and education in many poorer countries. This fact is reflected in increased longevity and reduced illiteracy. Much more remains to be done, but progress is not only possible but also actually occurring.

• • • • • • • • • • • • • • • • • • • • • • • • •

*Bibliography*

*Catechism of the Catholic Church*, pt. 3, sec. 2, chap. 2, art. 7, pars. 2401–63.
Pope John Paul II, *Veritatis Splendor* (1993).

## For Review

1. Why should we help the poor?

2. What are we to do with our riches? What is Christ's attitude to wealth?

3. List the Beatitudes. What is their point?

## Consider These

1. Our country is blessed with abundant resources. How can we help the poor? Do you know much about poor people in other countries? What is the Catholic Church doing to help in these countries?

2. Should the government do more than it is currently doing to help the poor here and overseas?

3. Pope John Paul II's encyclical *Veritatis Splendor* begins with the story of a rich young man. Is this story applicable to young men and women today?

4. Is there more happiness in giving than in receiving?

## Extension Exercises

1. Find out about the Saint Vincent de Paul Society or other Catholic organizations that help the needy. In which ways do such charitable organizations help the poor?

2. Invite an aid or development worker to your school to tell you about his activities.

3. Master Eckhart (1260–1327) was a Dominican priest from the Rhineland area of Germany. An important theologian and mystic, his many writings provoked a deal of controversy. He wrote the following poem:

> And in every deed, however puny,
> that results in justice
> God is made glad,
> glad through and through.
> At such a time
> there is nothing in the core of the Godhead
> that is not tickled through and through
> and that does not dance for joy.
> And those who follow compassion
> find life for themselves,
> justice for their neighbour,
> and glory for God.
>
> You may call God love
> you may call God goodness
> but the best name for God is
> Compassion.

a. As this poem indicates, Master Eckhart believed that God is delighted with our acts of kindness. Do you agree? Why/why not?

b. Consider his words about the good effects on those who act kindly. Are these claims realistic and true to life? Give examples.

4. Listen to the music from the stage production *Les Miserables* by Claude-Michel Schonberg. Does it express well the plight of the poor? Can you suggest other music that does so?

# CHAPTER SEVEN

# What's Sex Got to Do with Love and Marriage?

*What forms does love take?*

These days, there is great confusion between sex and love. Though they have obviously got something to do with each other, many people find it difficult to separate one from the other. Furthermore, it has become increasingly difficult to stick to one's own principles, to stand away from the crowd. How can we develop principles that will help us in our most fundamental relationships?

**True Love**

Catholics believe in love. In fact, true love is at the heart of Christian teaching. Our Lord said, "This is my commandment, that you love one another as I have loved you" (John 15:9,12). Saint Paul wrote, "If I have not love . . . I am nothing" (1 Corinthians 13:1–4).

Another word for love is charity, which is one of the Christian virtues. It means that we love God above all things and our neighbors as we love ourselves. It is love that makes us do the right thing, not fear of punishment or hope for some sort of reward. True love makes us generous and friendly and brings us happiness and peace.

But as any young person knows, love has a variety of meanings, depending on who is using the word. It is important to be clear about these meanings. Real love is different from both passionate emotion ("being in love") and from everyday dutiful affection. This is what Saint Paul meant when he wrote, "charity is patient and kind, charity is not jealous or boastful; it is not arrogant or rude. Charity does not insist on its own way" (1 Corinthians 13:4–7). Real love involves the will as well as the emotions, which is why it is so different from the "love" found in pop songs.

There are claims that the initial period of passionate love never lasts more than a couple of years. After that time, in good marriages, real love develops from passionate love. In real love, the lover wants the best for the beloved, helps the beloved to grow and is helped in turn. Basically, Christian love is not selfish; it is not looking after oneself and ignoring the rest. And it does not use people.

A constant searching after the myth of eternal passionate love is a mistake that many people make. Living in a difficult situation at home, being unhappy or experiencing an emotional trauma can sometimes provoke a search for this sort of love. But the idea of an eternal passionate love is a flight from reality, an unattainable dream that the fantasy world of advertising, popular magazines and television soaps dishonestly presents to us.

Most marriages follow a cycle of four stages: falling in love, settling down, disillusionment and then reconciliation. The tendency to drift apart and to feel dissatisfied seems to happen in most if not all marriages at some stage. This is one reason why there are serious marriage vows and why prayer, common sense and perseverance surround the unselfish love at the heart of good marriages. You will see this if you think about some of the good marriages with which you are familiar. If more people held realistic expectations of marriage, and if they understood that there will be difficult times, the divorce rate would not be nearly so high.

A good preparation for a successful marriage is to have a wide variety of friends of both sexes. Another good idea may be to look closely at marriages that you know are successful and try to work out why they have been so.

**Love of God**

The two great commandments are love of God and love of neighbor. But the greatest of all is to love our unseen God (Matthew 22:37–40). What does this mean? It means that God must have his place in all our relationships and must be part of every love that we experience. Human loves are not enough on their own.

This means that sexual love, married love or even the best family love is not the ultimate love, because sometimes these loves can close out the wider community that real Christian love is meant to include. Sometimes, even God can be left out—and this is not what he intended.

When God comes first, it is much easier to transform our need-loves into gift-loves. Friends will not use each other up with this sort of love; possessive parents will make sacrifices for their children and will allow them to grow up and become independent; and the selfish marriage partner will become more sensitive and generous. Naturally, all of this will require a lot of practice: this sort of loving does not come easily because we are all born with original sin, which means that we all have an inclination toward selfishness. We all have to learn to be good. It takes time and is never easy.

**Chastity**

Another word for chaste is pure. It usually refers to someone who is virtuous, sexually decent. We are all called to be chaste, no matter whether we are married or single, a teenager, divorced or widowed. What the virtue of chastity requires from us is to make sure that our sexual appetites are rightly ordered and successfully integrated into our whole personality.

Sexuality is a very strong driving force in our lives and can easily burn out of control. Yet if it is controlled and focused, it enriches our personality and helps us in the wider search for love.

For Christians, the sexual instinct, which was created by God for a purpose, is good. Sexual activity is also a part of God's loving plan. For Catholics, it is an expression of married love. It is important to remember that sexual sins are not usually the worst sins, although the sexual abuse of minors or sexual abuse with violence are very serious crimes.

Our Lord's teachings on sex are strict, but he did not denounce human weakness in matters of sex in the way he fiercely condemned hypocrisy or the indifference of the wealthy to the poor. In the Old Testament law, a woman convicted of adultery was punished with death by stoning. John's Gospel (8:3–11) tells how our Lord saved one adulterous woman from a mob intent on killing her. When she was safe, Jesus said two things to her: first, "I do not condemn you", and then, "go and do not sin any more."

Chastity, the proper use of our God-given sexual instincts, requires the achievement of self-mastery. It can be a difficult thing to accomplish because each stage in life presents another part of the same struggle—some of these stages are particularly difficult, such as adolescence.

Catholic teaching on sexuality comes directly from our Lord himself and has stood the test of time for two thousand years. Throughout that time, people have seen that Christ's teaching is designed to prepare them for marriage and then protect the married state for life. It also protects the children born from each marriage.

Nevertheless, since the 1960s, there has been a sexual revolution throughout the Western world. Casual sex has been promoted. "If it feels good, do it", is one message of the world we live in. Another is: "as long as you don't hurt anyone else, there's nothing wrong with it." Young people are encouraged to experiment as though personal hurt is impossible. This philosophy has received massive promotion through the media, especially television, which is so accessible to all.

The ready availability of the contraceptive pill and the promotion of the use of condoms are part of this sexual revolution. The main purpose of contraceptives is to separate sexual activity from marriage and to destroy the link between sex and childbearing. In this, the sexual revolution has been spectacularly successful. But the best proof that such behavior is not part of God's plan for us is that sexual freedom has not increased happiness.

This sort of sexual activity has got little to do with real love, whereas sexual intercourse between husband and wife is an expression of God's love, a deeply personal and very human expression that comes from the lifelong commitment and the mutual self-giving of two people who are equal partners in the sacrament of matrimony. When put into this context, it is far easier to see why sex, in God's plan, is kept special for marriage.

Just as the neopagans (i.e., contemporary unbelievers who deny the existence of the one true God) of our world sneer at Christianity, we should put current philosophies to the test. Has the sum of human misery increased as a result of the sexual revolution? Has divorce increased? How does this affect children? Has the pill meant fewer abortions? Have sexually transmitted diseases decreased? Where has the AIDS virus come from? Why are increasing numbers of young people turning to drugs and running away from home? What does the appalling rate of youth suicide tell us? All of these queries lead to the most important question: What brings more happiness in the long run—self-indulgence or self-restraint?

## Lust

Lust is an unchecked sexual appetite, a desire that becomes overmastering, a bit like being greedy rather than just having a healthy appetite for food. People dominated by lust are not common but not rare either. Our popular press would not concede that there are such people, yet it is very fond of highlighting sexual scandals.

People would be outraged if school authorities encouraged the distribution of mild cigarettes to schoolchildren as an antidote to smoking strong cigarettes. We would also be outraged if marijuana were distributed by schools as an alternative to using heroin or cocaine, or if low-alcohol beer were distributed as an alternative to whisky.

However, in the area of sexual responsibility we find the most amazing double standards. Contraceptives are promoted as ways of practicing "sexual responsibility". It seems as if our community refuses to believe that young people can be sexually self-disciplined; or perhaps it does not want them to be so. Given the huge range of vested interests involved, from the pharmaceutical companies to the media, the latter is not unlikely.

The fact is that the so-called "condom culture" is an insult to young people, as it presumes that they have no moral standards and, indeed, no self-control or personal discipline. It may be time for young people to express their reluctance to mess up their own lives in the way that the purveyors of the sexual revolution have done.

Lust can become a learned habit. If selfish pleasure becomes the main purpose of sexual activity, it will become a problem, as this is not self-giving but mutual taking. When selfish pleasure is the priority, especially outside of marriage but even inside it too, the foundations are being laid for later irresponsibility and sometimes for addiction.

Addictive behavior, whether sexual or connected with drink or drugs, develops when a person wants to escape reality by repeating a pleasurable experience that may have relieved tension and anxiety in the short term. In the longer term, though, a different pattern develops. Life becomes more and more centered on anticipating the act, and the longing for this can be almost irresistible as each completed act deepens the psychological need. Thus, life can become a constant search for no-ties sexual pleasure.

Males seem to be more vulnerable to this kind of addiction. Such men, victims of their own addiction, are usually not interested in the feelings of their partners; they are also unlikely to appreciate their own responsibilities to their partners or to any children born of their unions.

## Saint Augustine

Saint Augustine lived centuries ago, but his story is astonishingly similar to many told these days. He was born in 354 and died in 430. He lived in the Roman Empire province of North Africa, where he became a Catholic bishop in the small town of Hippo. Saint Augustine is the greatest theologian of the first Christian millennium, and his autobiography, called *Confessions*, is the first autobiography in Western literature.

Brought up a Catholic by his mother, Saint Monica, Augustine gave up his religion as a young man. He lived in a time that was somewhat like ours—partly pagan and partly Christian, though the Christians then were more fiercely divided than we are today.

His autobiographical story is striking for its honesty, as he describes his search for fulfillment in sex and his unhappiness. When the crisis struck, he was sixteen, had left school and was unemployed. As he describes, "I could not distinguish the clear light of true love from the murk of lust. Love and lust seethed within me." Augustine rejected his mother's warnings against sexual misconduct as "womanish advice" and, as he explains, "used to pretend that I had done things I had not done at all". He says that he increasingly gave in to vice in order not to be despised.

Though he loved his friends, they were "of a most unfriendly sort, bewitching my mind in an inexplicable way". He even took pleasure "from the thrill of having partners in sin", such as when thieving. But none of this made him happy, and he describes how he was exhausted "in depravity" and surrounded by "jealousy and suspicion, fear, anger and quarrels".

His mother never ceased to pray for him. He joined a strange sect called the Manichees and continued his studies in Carthage, Rome and Milan. Then he lived with a woman for many years: "a bargain struck for lust, in which the birth of children is begrudged, though, if they come, we cannot help but love them."

In Milan, he went to the cathedral, where he heard a famous bishop named Saint Ambrose preaching. This was the catalyst that helped him to change his ways, although his transformation did not happen without a fierce struggle within himself. Approaching his conversion, he prayed "Make me pure, but not yet!" This prayer is still famous today. In the year 387, he was baptized a Catholic, along with his son Adeodatus, by Saint Ambrose in the Milan cathedral crypt.

## Men and Women

The first book of the Old Testament, called the Book of Genesis, tells us that men and women are created in the image of God (Genesis 1:27). They are equal in personal dignity but have significant differences that are physical, moral, psychological and spiritual. Most of these differences are not due to any sort of historical conditioning but are clearly part of a God-given pattern. Men and women complement each other, and their very differences help in the building of successful marriages.

Motherhood is an integral part of womanhood, and it allows women to reveal their genius in living unselfish lives of love and service to others. This often happens even when a woman may have led a selfish existence before becoming a mother. Today's society undervalues the gift of motherhood. But in his 1995 letter to women, Pope John Paul II wrote that mothers "become God's own smile upon the newborn baby".

The more aggressive nature of men means that they are usually well suited to protect women and to take a significant part in providing for the family. Again, this can mean great dedication and unselfishness and may also often happen even when the man may have led a selfish existence before marriage. Marriage, commitment and the responsibilities of children usually bring out the best in people, which can be seen clearly as part of God's plan for us.

So, truly human behavior follows the direction that nature indicates to us. In the Jewish Christian tradition, homosexual activity has never been legitimized (Genesis 19:1–29; Romans 1:24–27).

The Church teaches that homosexual acts are intrinsically disordered and that they are against the law of God.

Homosexuals have been known in most cultures. Theirs is often a difficult life. They have every right to be respected and well treated, but their life-style should not be encouraged. In accordance with the Church's teachings, homosexual unions should not be given the same legal status as heterosexual marriages.

The psychological origins of homosexuality are disputed, though there are plenty of different theories as to whether homosexuals are "born" or "made". Some might be profoundly inclined toward homosexuality in their genetic makeup, but most homosexuals have learned this behavior and become bound to it by habit and the complexities of their life-style. Isolated homosexual experiences, especially in adolescence, need not mean that a person is destined to lead a homosexual life-style from then on; nor need they mean that a person has a truly homosexual orientation. Homosexuality is often presented as a respectable life-style by those who seek approval, not simply toleration. This is unchristian, and, in these times of the AIDS epidemic, it is dangerous.

In conclusion, sex and love really are integrally linked. The greatest happiness will come when sex is used as an expression of real love and kept for the confines of marriage. Young people are perfectly capable of high moral standards and of experiencing that real love that is God-given and God-centered.

## Bibliography

*Catechism of the Catholic Church*, pt. 3, sec. 2, arts. 6 and 9, pars. 2331–2400, 2514–33.

## For Review

1. What is meant by chastity? How does it differ from lust?

2. Is true love central to any discussion of sexuality?

3. How is the story of Saint Augustine relevant to us today?

• • • • • • • • • • • • • • • • • • • • • • • •

## Consider These

1. What is a good way of describing the Catholic attitude toward sex before marriage to a friend who has no religious beliefs?

2. Is chastity impossible in today's world?

3. Is the slogan "safe sex" a dangerous myth? Why/why not?

4. Why does the Catholic Church aim to protect the institutions of marriage and family? In what ways does her teaching reflect this stance?

• • • • • • • • • • • • • • • • • • • • • • • •

## Extension Exercises

1. Music can express both sacred, pure-hearted love and profane lust. For example, the "Liebstod" duet between Tristan and Isolde in the last act of Richard Wagner's (1813–1883) opera *Tristan and Isolde* displays the deep and abiding love between the characters. Which music do you consider expresses the high ideals of deep love between a man and a woman?

2. Conduct a survey of five popular magazines and summarize the attitudes found in them toward sex and teenagers. Do these attitudes help or hinder human development?

3. Is the traditional Christian opposition to homosexuality soundly based in terms of health? Is it charitable? Is there a difference between "homophobia" and objecting to homosexual activity? If so, explain these differences.

# CHAPTER EIGHT

# The Catholic Priesthood: What's It All About?

*What are the qualities of a good priest?*

The task of forming one's conscience and sticking to one's beliefs is often difficult. But God does not ask these difficult things of us in a vacuum. He gives us some powerful aids. Our priests are one such help. What is a priest, and how does he play his part in God's plan for redemption?

**The Catholic Priest**

The priest is a baptized man who has received the sacrament of holy orders. He has been ordained to priesthood in a special ceremony "to feed the Church by the word and grace of God"; consecrated for a special mission, he builds up the people of God and works for the salvation of others. Saint John Vianney was the parish priest of Ars, a small village in France. He explained the priesthood like this: "The priest continues the work of redemption on earth. . . . If we really understood the priest on earth, we would die not of fright but of love. The priesthood is the love of the heart of Jesus."

Through the sacrament of ordination, the priest receives a sacred power and his soul is marked or characterized in a new and permanent way. He becomes forever a representative of Christ, the Head of the Church. Christ acts through him. The priest is also able, through the power of the Holy Spirit, to represent the people before God, and especially to present to God the prayers of all the congregation when he celebrates the Eucharist.

There are two degrees of ministerial participation in the priesthood of Christ: bishops and priests. Deacons are not priests, but they do constitute one of the three orders of the sacred ministry and therefore receive the diaconate from the bishop.

## Redemption

All is not well in our world. There are wars, violence, starvation, sickness, premature death, families torn apart. The world needs a savior, a redeemer, someone to set things right. Christ our Lord did this through his death and Resurrection, but his victory will be complete only when suffering is banished on the last day. In other words, Jesus Christ, son of Mary and Son of God, truly human and truly divine, died on the Cross so that our sins could be forgiven. As the suffering servant, Christ showed God's love for us and unleashed the spiritual energy that empowers us to do good and lead lives of faith and service. Heaven, an eternity of happiness with God, becomes possible for us through this sacrifice.

Because of all this, Christ is the one mediator between God and man, our supreme High Priest. Christ's priesthood is shared and continued among us in two complementary ways: through baptism and confirmation, the whole community of believers participates in the priesthood of the faithful. The baptized are not only "God's own people" but are also a priestly people.

The ministerial or hierarchical priesthood of bishops and priests is essentially different from this common priesthood. Indeed, the ministerial priesthood exists to serve the common priesthood and especially to help unfold and develop the baptismal grace of all Christians. Through this means, Christ builds up the Church community.

### New Testament Leadership

Jesus himself chose his leaders, a small inner circle of disciples, whom he called apostles (those sent on mission). They were to be "fishers of men" or "shepherds" and became his representatives. In some mysterious way, these apostles were almost identified with the Christ who sent them out, and they served the other disciples. The role of the apostles was to preside over worship, to teach and to provide discipline for the community—what we now describe in theological terms as the offices of priest, prophet and king.

There were twelve apostles chosen during Christ's lifetime, but apostleship was later extended. Saint Paul, who, like the Twelve, was also called by Christ to be an ambassador (2 Corinthians 5:20), was the most famous addition (Galatians 1:1). There were further extensions of apostleship: "assistant" apostles (such as Barnabas and Silas, who were in direct contact with the original Twelve) and apostolic delegates (such as Timothy). People were brought into these positions in the later years of the apostolic generation. They acted as regional representatives of the apostles for a particular number of local churches. Their tasks were to maintain the teaching of the apostles (2 Timothy 4:1–5) and to organize the local ministry, whom they ordained or enrolled as officials (1 Timothy 3:1–13).

The terminology used for Church officials other than apostles varies throughout the New Testament. There were also local differences in patterns of leadership, although the evidence for this is not complete. Sometimes, those placed by the apostles in positions of local leadership were called "leaders" or "presidents in the Lord". More frequently, they were called presbyters or elders, bishops or overseers, and deacons. In many local churches without an apostle, there were colleges of presbyters (or groups of elders), like similar bodies in the Jewish synagogue. The relationship between these presbyters and the bishop (or overseer), who supervised the entire presbyterium, is not clear-cut.

The New Testament reveals the beginnings of the present Church order of bishop, priest and deacon. The Scriptures are always to be read in the light of Catholic tradition, recognizing the Church's ongoing authority to teach and to decide. It is Catholic teaching that our Lord instituted the apostles as an effective sign of his continuing authority in the Church. The apostles brought into being the ordained ministry, which applied and inherited the apostolic ministry itself. In other words, the ordained ministry is sacramentally rooted in the ministry of the apostles, and the bishops, as heads of the local churches, are the successors of the apostles.

## Jesus Ordains

We have seen how Jesus chose the twelve apostles as leaders (Matthew 10:1–5), gave them authority and sent them out to teach and heal, later giving a similar if lesser authority to the seventy-two disciples to work for the kingdom (Luke 10:1). However, it is official Catholic teaching, as defined by the whole Church at the Council of Trent in 1562, that Jesus ordained the apostles priests when he instituted the Eucharist at the Last Supper on the night before he died. He commanded them: "Do this as a memorial of me" (Luke 22:19; 1 Corinthians 11:24), thus ordaining them by word alone.

There is also considerable evidence in the New Testament, especially as the Christian communities spread and leadership passed to the first generation after the apostles, that the new leaders were commissioned (i.e., ordained) by a liturgical ceremony involving prayer and the laying on of hands (1 Timothy 4:14;

2 Timothy 1:6). When the early Christian community in Jerusalem elected the seven deacons to assist the apostles, "they presented these to the apostles, who prayed and laid their hands on them" (Acts 6:6).

## Unmarried Priests

Priests of the Latin rite (or family) of the Catholic Church are celibate and unmarried, although priests of the Eastern Catholic rites can marry before ordination. There are some exceptions to the Latin rite discipline, as married convert priests from the Anglican Church have been ordained and work as Catholic priests. Latin rite priests follow the example of Christ, who did not marry. This is a sacrifice of something good, not an avoidance of evil. Respect for celibacy and esteem for marriage reinforce one another.

Priestly celibacy "for the sake of the kingdom of heaven" (Matthew 19:12) means that the priest's heart should be undivided, given to God and his works, and turned away from the loves for wife and children. In an age like ours, which devalues sex by separating it from marriage and family, faithful celibacy asserts that the highest model of love is not sexual union but loving union with God.

Even when the Church has been stained with sexual scandals, when magazines proclaim that celibacy is impossible, probably unhealthy and somehow conducive to sexual deviancy, faithful priestly celibacy is still a superb and provocative witness to people inside and outside the Church. It remains the best sign that the priest has not signed up for some human advantage, real or imagined. The overwhelming majority of priests remain faithful to their promises, and the absence of family responsibilities can bring a radical freedom for service and hard work.

The present vitality of Catholic communities throughout the world is due in no small measure to the sacrifices of celibate priests, nuns and brothers. The history of the Western world cannot be understood without acknowledging the civilizing power of Catholic celibacy and understanding the freedom celibacy can bring in times of crisis. A single woman or man without family responsibilities is more able to die for a cause. Saint Maximilian Kolbe, a Franciscan priest, provides an example of such dedication: he died in a World War II German death camp as a result of compassionately volunteering to swap with a married man who had been selected for execution by starvation.

A good priest is a man for others because holy orders, like marriage, is a sacrament for others. Just as Christ was seen as the suffering servant who redeemed his people, so the priest must be, in some sense, like an Easter victim, a burnt offering. This does not mean that the priest must be regularly unhappy or bitter, but it does mean that the priest should be like a candle that is gradually used up, turned by God into light and love.

Such celibacy represents an awe-inspiring triumph over natural instincts and has ignited millions of souls with the love of God over the centuries. People recognize and admire such genuine sacrifice. It also helps to explain the priesthood and is one of the glories of Christendom, but only for people who understand something of faith and sacrifice.

## Mixed Tradition

Naturally, all people who are celibate are required to follow the general Christian prescriptions and practice continence or purity, that is, not engage in sexual activity. This is especially true of priests. Nevertheless, there certainly have been married clergy. We know that Saint Peter was married because our Lord cured Saint Peter's mother-in-law (Luke 4:38–39). There is no scriptural evidence on the marital status of the other apostles. Tradition tells us that Saint John was unmarried and that Saint Philip the apostle and Philip (one of the seven first deacons) were both married with daughters.

Paul's first letter to Timothy lists the criteria for a bishop, including the necessity of not being married more than once (1 Timothy 3:1–7). However, there were early Christian traditions, probably stemming from Jewish customs as well as from our Lord's personal practice, that saw celibacy and purity as appropriate for priests.

Even in early times different emphases appeared in Eastern and Western Christianity. These days, the Orthodox Church has married priests as well as celibate monks and bishops. In the early Church in the East and the West, priests could marry before ordination. This right was recognized explicitly by the Synod of Trullo in Constantinople in 692 after the sixth General Council.

The Council of Nicaea in 325, the first great meeting of all the world's bishops in the Roman Empire, refused to outlaw married clergy. But from at least the fourth century, and probably even from apostolic times, especially in the West, sexual abstinence was required not only of single clergy but also of those who were married. They were to live with their wives as "brother and sister" (as, for example, Pope Siricius in 386 and Pope Leo the Great in 458 taught).

Efforts continued throughout the Middle Ages to maintain the norm of celibacy for clergy. The Second Lateran Council of 1139 made the marriage of clergy invalid as well as unlawful. When the Protestant and Anglican Churches broke away during the sixteenth century Reformation and allowed the clergy to marry, the Catholic Church, through the Council of Trent (1545–1463), reaffirmed the discipline of clerical celibacy. This is basically the situation today.

## Priest Shortage

Could the discipline of the Western Church change? Would not allowing priests to marry remove the shortage of clergy? Jesus said that "a good tree brings forth good fruit" (Matthew 7:17). If we continue strong in faith and service, God will continue to look after the centerpiece of his kingdom, namely, the Catholic Church. God will provide, sometimes in ways we do not expect.

Our country is not lacking in Catholic priests in relation to many other countries. However, many dioceses have a critical shortage of seminarians (men studying to become priests). This is not a worldwide pattern, as today there are more than twice the number of diocesan seminarians as when Pope John Paul II was elected in 1978. But a scarcity of seminarians is a fact in many parts of the Western world.

The Church now spells out more clearly the religious responsibilities of lay people. Because the hostile pressures on faith and religious practice are stronger than ever, greater lay involvement in Church communities will be required.

The answer to the vocations crisis depends on the strength of the Catholic community's faith and the generosity of young people. The Church remains irrevocably committed to the necessity of the sacraments and local priestly leadership. However, because priestly celibacy is a matter of discipline and not of faith or morals, the Church could, in the future, allow the ordination of married men. But there is no indication that the Church will allow this in the near future and no certainty that such a provision would help strengthen religious vitality in the long run. Our religious problems and the decline of faith and practice may well prove to be immune to attempts to improve religious vitality based merely on disciplinary changes.

## Clergy and Laity

Some claim that our parishes could follow the trend in Catholic schools, with priests being replaced by lay leaders as many brothers and sisters have been replaced by lay teachers. This minority sometimes appeals to the Second Vatican Council (1962–1965), when the Pope and bishops gathered together in Rome to reorient the Church for the future. But the supporters of lay leaders give little evidence of having read the documents. Certainly, Vatican II issued a special decree on the role of the laity, stressing their baptismal dignity and their responsibilities in the world. Within the Church, this encouragement of the laity saw the establishment of parish councils, parish finance committees, school boards, and even diocesan pastoral councils.

In the Catholic scheme of things, both laity and clergy are essential. But they play complementary roles, however, and are not alternatives. The clergy are as necessary as lay people. Early in the second century, Saint Ignatius, Bishop of Antioch, wrote that without the bishop, presbyters and deacons, "one cannot speak of the Catholic Church" (*Ad Trall.* 3:1). In some places, there are parishes and Mass centers without a resident priest. However, strictly speaking, there can be no such thing as a "priestless parish" where priestly activity is entirely absent. Such a situation would be a contradiction in terms because priestly religious leadership is essential for the sacraments and for other more general matters in all Catholic parishes.

*Bibliography*

*Catechism of the Catholic Church*, pt. 2, sec. 2, chap. 3, art. 6.

## For Review

1. What is a Catholic priest?

2. List the things that only a priest can do.

3. Explain how Jesus himself ordained priests.

• • • • • • • • • • • • • • • • • • • • • • • •

## Consider These

1. What are the priesthood's greatest challenges?

2. Do you think that the modern world is hostile to the idea of priesthood? Explain your reasons.

3. Why is it difficult to become a priest? Why is the training so lengthy?

4. What can the Catholic lay person do to help priests?

5. Consider why there is a decline in vocations in some parts of the world and yet a rise in vocations in many poor countries.

6. Is a priest different from a social worker or lecturer? In what ways?

7. In what ways are nuns similar to, or different from, priests?

• • • • • • • • • • • • • • • • • • • • • • • •

## Extension Exercises

1. Ask a young priest of your acquaintance why he chose to be a priest. Why do you think young men still become priests?

2. Graham Greene's *The Power and the Glory* (1940) is a famous novel about a whiskey priest on the run during the 1920s anti-Catholic persecutions in Mexico. Read chapter 2. Why was the wine so important to the fugitive priest?

3. There are over 400,000 Catholic priests throughout the world. They do many different types of priestly work, as shown in books such as the following: Donald Cave's *Percy Jones: Priest, Musician, Teacher* (1988); Tom Prior's *A Knockabout Priest* (1985); the story of prison chaplain Father John Brosnan; and Father Ernie Smith's autobiographical *Miracles Do Happen: A Priest Called Smith* (1993). Study one book or article on a priest, from history or from today. Does this article conform to your impression of a priest and his work? Explain your answer.

# CHAPTER NINE

# Why Can't Catholic Women Be Priests?

By G. Pell with A. Krohn and M. H. Woods

*What do you know about the role of women in the Church?*

Many different denominations allow women to be pastors or priests. Some, including the Catholic Church, do not. What are the reasons for this? Why does the Catholic Church hold strongly to her traditional stance?

### Catholic Teaching

The official Catholic teaching is that the Church does not have the power to ordain women as priests because Jesus and the apostles did not authorize their ordination (a constant Church teaching for nearly two thousand years). In May 1994, Pope John Paul II restated the Church's definitive teaching on this matter. In November 1995, the Congregation for the Doctrine of the Faith (the highest Vatican teaching agency) explained that this limitation is an infallible teaching.

## Catholic Priesthood

The Church teaches that priests are religious leaders because they represent Christ, the Head of the Church. Bishops, who have the fullness of the priesthood, are symbols of God the Father. However this leadership must be seen as Christian service; it is not a power game.

Ministerial priesthood is received by a special sacrament that goes back to the time of Christ and the apostles, so the priest's status is different from that of the baptized, who are made like Christ through baptism but do not share the priest's type of religious leadership. The baptized share the priesthood of all God's people. Priests and people need one another to praise God and for the service of society.

The priest is an ambassador of Christ, who is the Head of the Church. The priest's ordination, which is a gift from the Holy Spirit, gives him special powers that are used to celebrate the Eucharist, forgive sins and anoint the sick. He will also usually baptize the faithful and bless their marriages. He is ordained to minister to the faithful, to serve and to help. Above all, the priest must regularly preach Christ's "good news", or the gospel, the whole of it, whether people are interested or not, and he must pray for all his people as he prays for himself.

We must not forget that in the Mass, the priest is not just leading the people in commemorating Jesus' life and death but also makes present again Jesus' sacrifice on the Cross by changing the bread and wine into Jesus' Body and Blood. This stupendous miracle is possible because through ordination the priest is identified with Christ—"This is my Body, this is my Blood", he prays at the consecration.

The male priest is an icon (part image, part representative) of Christ, which is appropriate. It would be inappropriate for a woman to represent Christ, just as it would be inappropriate for a male to represent our Lady.

## Priestesses

The pagans of ancient Greece and Rome worshipped many gods and goddesses from about 1000 B.C. to A.D. 400. (Pagans are people who do not acknowledge the one true God.) These deities were given human form. Usually the goddesses, such as Artemis (Diana for the Romans), Aphrodite (Venus) and Nike (Victory), were served by priestesses, although the goddess Athena was an exception. However, both priests and priestesses were active in some temples. Priestesses were particularly common among the ancient Greeks. The Vestal virgins, whose circular temple was in the Roman forum, were the most important Roman priestesses. Usually six in number and vowed to virginity, they supervised the cult of Vesta, the hearth goddess. Their principal task was to keep alive the sacred flame. Vestals convicted of impurity were entombed alive, but there are only twenty recorded examples of this in their history, which extends over one thousand years of dedicated (although misguided) service.

The Jews were strongly opposed to paganism and priestesses, and faithful Jews had to struggle regularly to resist those influences. Pagan priestesses, therefore, were quite common in our Lord's time.

## Ways of Thinking

In reaching conclusions on important religious issues, Catholics first of all look at what Jesus and his chosen leaders, the apostles, taught and what they did in practice. We discover this in the Scriptures—especially the New Testament—which are called "the Word of God" because their content was revealed by God himself. Secondly, we look at the teachings and practices of the Church during her two-thousand-year history, especially the teachings of the popes, councils, bishops and the great theologians and religious writers. In other words, on important religious issues, Catholics do not decide matters by holding a referendum or by finding out what seems just or unjust or what is the most "up-to-date" view but by examining what Christ and the apostles taught and did and what the Church teaches.

The Catholic Church has many doctrines that are easily understood, such as those relating to love and compassion for the poor and suffering. But she also has teachings that are seen as difficult and unpopular; for example, the Church is against divorce and remarriage, teaches that the body and blood of Christ are really present in the Eucharist, is opposed to abortion and artificial contraception and calls us to forgive others always. The Church can afford to run the risks and pay the price of short-term unpopularity because she is more than human. The Church is rooted in the divine, the supernatural.

## No Injustice

It is not unjust that women cannot become Catholic priests, because no person has a right to be a priest. The priesthood is a vocation, or calling, from God. Jesus, unlike the Jewish rabbis of his time, chose his disciples and especially the leaders (Matthew 4:18–22; Mark 3:13–14)—"It was not you who chose me, but I who chose you" (John 15:16).

We should remember that the priesthood is not a secular job or a means to a career path. Life is full of mysteries: Why are some people more beautiful than others, more athletic, more intelligent? Is this unjust?

Although the one great God is a spirit, neither male nor female, Jesus told us to call God our Father (Matthew 6:9), and the Word of God came among us as a man, Jesus of Nazareth, who described himself as a bridegroom to his people (Matthew 9:15). Saint Paul also compared the love of Christ for his Church to the love of a husband for his wife (Ephesians 5:31–32). With this background, in which God became man and Jesus' preferred term for God was "Father", it is easier to understand why Jesus followed the Jewish traditions, rejecting the practices of the surrounding pagans, and chose only men to continue to represent him as priests. The male imagery used in Jesus' description of God as "Father" gives Christians a unique insight into the nature of God. In short, then, if we have a problem with injustice, we must have this argument with Jesus! The basic question is not whether women should be priests but whether we trust Jesus' teaching and practice.

## Types of Feminism

Feminism is behind the call for women priests. But there are several different kinds of feminism. Some Catholic feminists simply wish to uphold the equal dignity and importance of women and believe that a more positive understanding of women's ministries should be made. They do not disagree with the Catholic teaching on the priesthood. Other Christian feminists are reformers who are campaigning for equality in the Church by altering the language of the liturgy and the nature of the priesthood. They may not realize that these proposed changes go far beyond the social changes of equal opportunity and call into question the foundational beliefs of Christianity. Yet another group of feminists within the Church use the assumptions of revolutionary secular humanism, which aim to destroy belief in the one true God, to measure the claims of Christianity. They believe that males have conspired over hundreds of years to use institutions such as the family and the Church as a means of silencing and oppressing women. Their intention is not just to install women at the altar but to destroy the beliefs that the Word of God became a man and that God should be described as a Trinity of Father, Son and Holy Spirit. They want to redefine radically Church teaching on human life and sexual morality and would create a new and unrecognizable "Woman Church". Finally, there are feminists who are either ex-Christians or non-Christians and who are very vocal in their support of women's ordination.

Many of these people are opposed to Christianity and want to replace it with a woman-centered paganism.

## Scripture Teaching

Nobody claims that Jesus left a blueprint for every small development, but like every great leader, he had clear ideas on basic issues, such as ordaining women as priests. Jesus showed a freedom, kindness and respect for women that was unusual in the Jewish customs of the times. For example, according to the custom of the time, he should not have spoken publicly to the Samaritan woman by the well (John 4:27), he allowed a sinful woman to anoint his feet in the house of Simon the Pharisee (Luke 7:38), and he forgave the woman accused of adultery (John 8:11). Women had a special place in his life and work. A group of women accompanied Jesus and the Twelve on their missionary journeys (Luke 8:2–3), and our Lord appeared first to a woman after his Resurrection (John 20:11–18).

Despite this, Jesus did not appoint any women to the Twelve, nor did he ordain any women to celebrate the Eucharist or to forgive sins. Neither did he authorize his apostles to ordain women. Even after the disgrace of Judas Iscariot, our Lady, who had an honored place in the early Christian community, was not chosen as a replacement apostle; neither were any of the strong women who followed him to the foot of the Cross.

Naturally, women were a large and valued part of the first Christian communities. They were encouraged to pray aloud and prophesy in church. However, they were forbidden by Saint Paul to preside or to teach officially during the liturgical services (1 Corinthians 14:34–35; 1 Timothy 2:12).

## Fundamentals

It is interesting to note that most Catholic women throughout the world support the Church's teaching on priesthood. They realize their lives can be just as significant and influential in God's plan. Advocacy for women priests is strongest in the English-speaking world. Male resistance to the idea of women priests appears rarely to be based on fear but rather on theological and scriptural grounds.

Catholics have always believed in fundamentals because the Church has to mean what she says and say what she means. This is why we have creeds and baptismal promises. But Catholics are not fundamentalists—the Church encourages people to consider the context of scriptural passages, the importance of the text and the teaching of the Church, not to adhere literally and unthinkingly to their private interpretation of the Scriptures.

All Christians are bound by Scripture. We are not free to reject those bits we do not like, but understanding Scripture is difficult and can be done safely only with the help of the teaching Church.

## No Change Possible

The official teaching of the Catholic Church has never varied from the beginning of Christianity to the time of Pope John Paul II: the Church cannot ordain women to the priesthood because she does not have the power to ordain women. The Church must remain faithful to the example of our Lord and the apostles, who did not admit women to the Twelve, did not ordain them to celebrate the Eucharist and did not authorize their successors to do so. So, based on the past, women's ordination can never happen in the future. Some Catholics resent this fact being spelled out, but it is better to explain the official teaching and its basic consequences rather than to allow people to be confused.

A few heretical sects have attempted something like women's ordination (for example, the Marcionites and Montanists in the second century and the Catharists and Waldensians in the Middle Ages). More recently, some Protestant and Anglican churches have admitted women into their ministries. However, their ideas of ministry and priesthood are often different from the Catholic viewpoint. The Orthodox Churches certainly have real or valid sacraments, clergy and bishops. They too do not believe they have the power to ordain women as priests.

## Marian Devotion

Mary, the Mother of God, is certainly a problem for some feminists. But she is a marvelous role model for both men and women in their relationship with God. Pope John Paul II says that "the nature of woman includes a special bond to the Mother of the Savior." Throughout history, Marian devotion has not oppressed women but rather has encouraged them to their highest dignity. In the Mother of God, women have a model who cannot be surpassed by any man.

Only Mary was immaculate, and she will always be our greatest saint. Our Lady also reminds us that a person does not have to be a priest to be a good Catholic and that priesthood is not the only significant form of Christian service.

• • • • • • • • • • • • • • • • • • • • • • • •

*Bibliography*

*Catechism of the Catholic Church*, pt. 2, sec. 2, chap. 3, art. 6, especially par. 1577.

## For Review

1. What does the Catholic Church teach about women and priesthood?

2. Give some of the reasons for this teaching.

3. Is the role of women in the Catholic Church inferior to or different from that of men?

## Consider These

1. Most professions are open to men and women. What makes the priesthood different? Why is tradition so important to the Church?

2. We have rights and responsibilities in some areas but not in others. Why is it that no one, regardless of his gender, has a right to priesthood?

## Extension Exercises

1. Explore Luke's Gospel; to discover Jesus' attitude toward women, especially chapters 1, 2 and 7.

2. a. Has any other institution in human history given as many leadership opportunities to women as the Catholic Church?

   b. Is it true that until the Second Vatican Council (1962–1965), nearly all Catholic primary schools, most Catholic secondary schools and Catholic hospitals were led by women?

c. Was the leadership of Blessed Mary McKillop (1842–1909), who is the only Australian to be beatified by the Catholic Church, unusual or were all religious orders for women run by women?

d. What were the attributes and contributions of Saint Frances Xavier Cabrini and Saint Elizabeth Ann Seton that led to their canonization? What was unique about them?

# CHAPTER TEN

# Peter the Rock: What Is the Pope's Role Today?

*What would you say to the Pope if you ever had the opportunity to speak with him?*

The ministerial priesthood and the lay faithful make up the people of God. But at the head of this whole huge Catholic Church sits one solitary man, the pope. How did one man get such responsibility? What does the pope mean in our lives?

### The Role of the Pope

The title "pope" comes from the Greek word *pappas*, which means, literally, "papa". It is now used to designate the leader of the Catholic Church throughout the world. The pope is the world's chief witness of God crucified and risen in Christ Jesus. His unique office was first transmitted by our Lord himself to Saint Peter, the leader of the apostles, so that the pope is the successor of Saint Peter and bishop of the Church of Rome. He is head of the College of Bishops and pastor of the universal Church on earth. Known since the sixth century as the Servant of the Servants of God, and since the thirteenth century as the Vicar of Christ, the pope is the successor of Saint Peter; he is united as one with the other bishops, successors of the apostles, in the College of Bishops.

The office of the papacy, strengthened by the Holy Spirit, is much more than the individual capacity of any one pope, no matter how saintly or capable he might be. It is also a mystery of faith; sometimes a sign of contradiction. The papacy was a principal point of division in the split with the Orthodox Churches in 1054 and when Protestant communities broke away in the Reformation of the sixteenth century.

The pope is the centerpiece of the huge mosaic of different Catholic communities across the continents, now numbering 950 million people. Over the centuries, this leadership has been exercised in different ways and has been accepted or resisted to different degrees by the local churches. Opinions about the popes differ among us too.

Some popes have been saints, most have been capable religious leaders; some were inept, a few were public sinners. But the office is more important than the person, and the office remains, no matter how deficient the officeholder. Each pope is called to be the public champion of the Catholic tradition and the best-known symbol and protector of Church unity.

Opponents of the Church realize, often better than Catholics, the strengths of Church unity. Conquerors and tyrants feared and opposed the papacy. Napoleon imprisoned two popes, Pius VI and Pius VII, before he was defeated by the Quadruple Alliance in 1815. Hitler boasted at table that when he won the Second World War he would destroy the papacy and set up a pope in each country. In every nation the communists took over, they tried to set up a national Catholic Church and separate bishops, priests and people from the pope.

## The New Testament on Peter

Saint Peter played an important role among Jesus' followers before and after the Resurrection. Originally called Simon, the son of Jonah, he was a married man and a fisherman from Bethsaida on the north bank of the Sea of Galilee. The brother of Andrew, he was among the first to be chosen by our Lord; in fact, he became the principal disciple as leader of the twelve apostles and one of the inner circle of three with James and John. His family home was Jesus' base in Capernaum.

Loyal, impetuous and outspoken, probably a born leader, his faults are also recorded vividly in the Scriptures. His celebrated denial during the Passion that he knew Jesus is nearly as infamous as Judas' betrayal. He objected strongly to the prospect of Jesus' suffering and dying. He was not at the foot of the Cross.

It was our Lord who renamed Simon as Peter, "the man of rock", on whom Jesus would build the Church that would never fail. Peter shared the solidity and stability of the one true God who is our fortress and our rock. Jesus also gave him the keys of the kingdom of heaven and the power to permit and forbid, to acquit and condemn (Matthew 16:18–19). Just before the Passion, Luke describes our Lord prophesying Peter's denial, telling him that "once you have recovered, you in your turn must strengthen your brothers" (Luke 22:31–32). At the conclusion of John's Gospel, we also have the beautiful scene by the Sea of Tiberias when the risen Jesus asked Peter three times whether he loved him. Peter was upset by the repeated question and energetically protested his love. He was commanded to feed the Lord's lambs and his sheep (John 21:15–17), an instruction recalling Jesus' own parable of the good shepherd who lays down his life for his sheep (John 10:7–18).

It was Peter in particular who kept the followers of the Lord together in the aftermath of the Resurrection. He preached to the crowds after the coming of the Spirit at Pentecost and supervised the appointment of Matthias as the twelfth apostle to replace Judas Iscariot, the traitor who had committed suicide. Even Saint Paul, in his clash with Saint Peter, acknowledged Peter's special role as a pillar of the Church and preacher to the circumcised (Galatians 2:7–14).

**Bishop of Rome**

Although this fact is not recounted in the Scriptures, ancient tradition records that Saint Peter traveled to Rome, which was the capital of the Roman Empire, lived and worked with the Christian community, and was martyred there in the persecutions of the Emperor Nero between the years 64 and 68. Clement of Rome, writing later in the first century, speaks of this martyrdom (without placing it in Rome).

From at least the middle of the second century, Christians have revered a tomb in the pagan burial grounds near Nero's Circus as the burial place of Peter. The earliest Christian Emperor, Constantine (306–337), built the first Saint Peter's Church directly over this tomb. Today, the main altar of Saint Peter's Basilica and Bernini's baldachino in Rome are still directly above this tomb, which can be visited below the present church in the recent excavations. Saint Paul also came to the center of the known world to preach the gospel of Christ.

Early in the second century, the martyr Ignatius, bishop of Antioch, acknowledged the preeminence of the church in Rome "presiding in love", and her teachers Peter and Paul (Romans 4:3). Later in the second century (c. 190) another bishop, Irenaeus of Lyons, spoke of the Roman church founded by Peter and Paul as the fullest example of the apostolic faith, which he praised for being better preserved there than anywhere else (*A.H.* III 3:1–3). Catholics believe that Peter, the leader of the apostles and chosen by Christ himself, also became leader of the Christians in the city of Rome. Later bishops of Rome saw themselves as succeeding to his position. There is no doubt that Paul's presence in Rome also enhanced the prestige of the church of Rome and her bishops, just as the whole Church's understanding of the teachings of Scripture about the Petrine ministry has developed over the centuries.

It is for these historical reasons that the pope will always be bishop of Rome, even if he is unable to live in that city. In 1303 King Philip IV of France kidnapped Pope Boniface VIII, who died during this captivity. Then Boniface IX took up residence in Perugia, and the next pope lived in Avignon. Some later popes also came from here. Finally in 1377, Saint Catherine of Siena persuaded Pope Gregory XI to return and live in Rome. From 1378 to 1417, Avignon claimed a separate papacy of popes who were mainly of French origin. This period is known as the Great Schism. It finally ended when three rival popes were forced to abdicate and Pope Martin V was universally recognized.

## Choosing the Pope

The pope is chosen by the College of Cardinals, who since 1059 have been the exclusive electors of the Holy Father. The cardinals are ranked immediately after the pope and chosen by him. Originally, all cardinals lived and worked in Rome with the pope, but since the twelfth century they have also been chosen from outside the city. They are senior Church leaders and the pope's advisers and chief administrators.

Their number was limited to thirty until the year 1686, when Pope Sixtus V increased the maximum to seventy. In 1965 Pope Paul VI ordered that on their eightieth birthday, cardinals lose the right to enter into the conclave (the meeting that elects the new pope), and in 1973 he set the maximum number of electors at 120. In November 1994 Pope John Paul II created thirty new cardinals from around the world, bringing the total number to 167; however, forty-seven were above the age limit set for electors. All cardinals are now bishops.

On the death of a pope, the cardinal electors meet in the Vatican's Sistine Chapel, which was built for Pope Sixtus IV (1471–1484) and later decorated by Michelangelo's magnificent frescoes, including his painting of the Last Judgment on the altar wall. Since 1271, when they had been unable to agree on a new pope after three years' deliberation, cardinals have been isolated from the world during the election. Regularly during an election, the progress is reported to the world by smoke: black smoke means no result yet, while white smoke signifies the choice of a new pope. A clear majority of votes (two-thirds plus one) is needed for a valid election.

## Many Different Popes

The total number is disputed, but officially Pope John Paul II is the 264th pope. Information is scarce on some of the popes in the tenth and eleventh centuries. There have been thirty-seven false or antipopes (whom the Church has not accepted as genuine), and there was no John XV (because historians were mistaken in believing that a mythical Pope John reigned for four months before the erroneously named John XVI) or a John XX.

More than one-third of the popes were Romans and another 40 percent were from Italy. The Dutchman Adrian VI (1522–1523) was the last non-Italian pope until Pope John Paul II from Poland was elected in 1978. Eight of the seventeen popes between the years 654 and 752 were Greek, and seventeen popes between the years 999 and 1378 were French. Pope Victor (189–198) was from northern Africa. He was the first Western or Latin-speaking pope to succeed the Easterners. One Englishman, Adrian IV (1154–1159), was pope. Between 537 and 1048, seven popes were deposed (i.e., removed from office by powerful rulers), and four popes have resigned from office, the last being Celestine V in 1294.

## Pope John Paul II

Pope John Paul II was born Karol Wojtyla on May 18, 1920, in Wadowice, southern Poland. His father was a retired army lieutenant, and his mother died when he was a small boy. He was a good athlete and scholar and a university student in Krakow when the Germans invaded Poland during the Second World War. He undertook forced labor in a quarry and then in a factory. After his father's death in 1942, he began studying secretly for the priesthood and was ordained in 1946, when he also published his first volume of poetry. He gained two doctorates and was appointed to teach ethics in Lublin.

By 1958 he was an auxiliary bishop in Krakow, and in 1963 he became archbishop there. Active at the Second Vatican Council and later synods, he cooperated with Cardinal Wyszynski of Warsaw to gain more freedom for the Church from the communist government of Poland. In 1978 he was elected pope. In 1981 he was shot and wounded by a terrorist in Saint Peter's Square in Rome.

A charismatic figure and a great traveler, Pope John Paul II has been seen in public by more people than any other human being in history. He played a prominent role in provoking the communist collapse in Europe in 1989 and has vigorously defended the essentials of Catholic teaching in faith and morals. He is one of the great popes of history.

## *Time* Magazine's Man of the Year, 1994

*Time* magazine explained its choice this way: "In a year when so many people lamented the decline in moral values or made excuses for bad behavior, Pope John Paul II forcefully set forth his vision of the good life and urged the world to follow. For such rectitude—or recklessness, as his detractors would have it—he is *Time*'s Man of the Year."

The Pope is the best-known messenger for all Christianity. He is not just the defender of Catholic doctrine but a moral compass for believers and nonbelievers alike. His is a message not of expedience or compromise but of right and wrong. Many young people in particular love the Pope because he speaks of hope when there is so much pessimism and so much fear for the future.

## The Infallibility of the Pope

The claim that the Catholic Church is infallible implies that, under specific conditions, the Church can certainly teach the truth. As the head of the Church, the pope articulates the faith of the Church. Dependent on the special protection of the Holy Spirit for the Church, the First Vatican Council in 1870 defined that when the pope, using his apostolic authority as head of the Church, teaches a doctrine of faith or morals to be held by all the faithful, his teachings cannot be in error. The 1950 dogma that our Lady was assumed body and soul into heaven is a clear example of a solemn and infallible teaching. There are many essential truths binding on Catholics that have not been defined infallibly, for example, the existence of the one, true God.

## A Unique Story

The history of the popes and the survival of the Catholic Church are extraordinary, in fact, unique. This fact is an additional argument supporting the Catholic Church's claim to be the one true church founded by Jesus Christ. The nineteenth-century English historian Lord Thomas Macaulay, who was often hostile to the Church, eloquently captured and conveyed the magnitude of this achievement in 1840:

> [The papacy] saw the commencement of all the governments and all the ecclesiastical establishments that now exist in the world; and we feel no assurance that she is not destined to see the end of them all. She was great and respected before the Saxon had set foot on Britain, before the Frank had passed the Rhine, when Grecian eloquence still flourished at Antioch, when the idols were still worshipped in the temple at Mecca. And she may still exist in undiminished vigor when some traveler from New Zealand shall, in the midst of a vast solitude, take his stand on a broken arch of London Bridge to sketch the ruins of Saint Paul's.

London Bridge has been carried off to Arizona, but the paragraph remains as a golden tribute to one of the Holy Spirit's most dazzling exploits.

• • • • • • • • • • • • • • • • • • • • • • • •

*Bibliography*

*Catechism of the Catholic Church*, especially pars. 442–43, 552–53, 880–85, 1443–45.

Kelly, J. N. D., *The Oxford Dictionary of Popes* (Oxford University Press, 1986).

## For Review

1. Explain the role of the pope.

2. The pope is said to be the bishop of Rome. Why Rome?

3. What is the scriptural foundation for the papacy?

## Consider These

1. Pope John Paul II has earned the respect of many of the world's leaders.

   a. Research the vision he has outlined for the members of the Catholic Church.

   b. Why was he made *Time* magazine's Man of the Year in 1994?

2. When was the Second Vatican Council? Which pope set it up? Why? What did it achieve? What are its lasting effects?

3. How important is the papacy in the life of the Church?

## Extension Exercises

1. Saint Leo the Great (440–461), Saint Gregory the Great (590–604) and Innocent III (1198–1216) are often rated among the greatest of the popes. What were their achievements?

2. a. There have been some notorious popes, for example: Alexander VI (1492–1503), who was the father of Lucretia and Cesare Borgia; and Julius II (1503–1513), who was the patron of Michelangelo and the last pope to lead the papal troops personally in battle. Are the actual histories as bad as the popular stories?

   b. Did history's infamous popes help to provoke the Protestant Reformation in the sixteenth century?

3. What are the names, backgrounds and achievements of the two popes who preceded Pope John Paul II?

4. Was there ever a Pope Joan?

# CHAPTER ELEVEN

# What Does It Mean to Be Female?

## By Mary Helen Woods

*What qualities is the artist Botticelli (1445–1510)
seeking to express?*

One of the great debates in modern times has been about the
changing role of women in today's society. While there is no doubt
that women's roles have changed significantly, there is much argument over how women (and men) understand their roles and priorities. The following three cases are examples of scenarios that
many women face.

**Case 1:** Melinda is in her last year at school and feels confused about all the messages she gets about how women are meant to behave. Some people suggest that she should be sexually carefree by using contraception and not feeling committed to any relationship. Others suggest that, as an adult, her ambitions should center around paid work and that the desire to be married with children is now just plain old-fashioned.

**Case 2:** Peter is a marketing manager who is doing reasonably well in his career. He is married to Julie, and they have two small children. Peter wants Julie to return to work because the second income will help them to improve their life-style. But Julie wants to be at home with her children until they are at school.

**Case 3:** Adriana is a young lawyer who has been offered a partnership in her legal firm. She is delighted by this but knows that work will now become more than a full-time commitment, leaving little time for other things. She is happily married and has been thinking of starting a family. She is torn between whether to postpone having children and accept the promotion or to begin her family soon.

When we are making the important decisions about how best to lead our lives, we need to have some broad goals. For Catholics, these are centered around the teachings of Jesus Christ, who made it clear that we have a specific destiny while on this earth. Edith Stein, a German Jewish philosopher who converted to Catholicism, became a Carmelite nun and was martyred at Auschwitz in a Nazi concentration camp, described our destiny this way: "to grow into the likeness of God through the development of our faculties, to procreate descendants, and to hold dominion over the earth". This destiny is the same for men as it is for women. But because men and women have been given different attributes by God, there will be differences in the way we achieve our destinies.

Men and women have many attributes in common, but women have as well special talents for caring and protecting.

Many women have the ability to create strong emotional links, are particularly good at adapting themselves to different circumstances and are capable of much unselfishness, altruism, strength and intelligence. It is fascinating to see how, despite the differences between men and women, they often complement each other.

The most perfect model of womanhood in Christian experience is God's mother, Mary. Though the Gospels tell us little about her, the images we have are extremely feminine ones. Think of her intelligent acceptance when it was revealed to her that she would become the Mother of God. Reflect on her concern when she could not find her small son. Consider her thoughtful intervention at the wedding feast at Cana. Think of her powerful influence over her son and others and of the love and dedication she lavished on both husband and son. Ponder her grief for her persecuted son and her pain at the foot of the Cross. Hers was a life encompassed by intelligent and enlightened faith, by love, humility, compassion, courage, strength and forgiveness. Clearly, God gave us his Mother as a role model and inspiration for our ideal of the feminine.

Yet the image of Mary the Mother of God seems not to be compatible with modern feminism. Is there a gulf between being feminine and being feminist? Is it time for a new role model that acknowledges and values all of women's gifts?

## History of Feminism

For centuries in Western society it was expected that women would become wives, mothers or nuns. As they grew up, girls were taught domestic skills such as weaving and cooking, worked alongside men in the fields, worked in cottage industries, or were initiated into religious practice in convents. But social development changed all this. During the Industrial Revolution, women were used as a cheap labor force and were compelled through economic circumstances to work outside the home. This had adverse effects on family life, so much so that the early British feminists campaigned to allow women to be at home with their families rather than be forced into paid work.

During the 1900s, domestic activities were gradually rede-
signed: much of the housework that had previously been done
laboriously by hand was mechanized. As further advances were
made, appliances such as washing machines, vacuum cleaners,
electric stoves, clothes driers and microwaves reduced the burden
of housework. Even for a large family, housework took up much
less time and effort. Women, who have always traditionally been
responsible for looking after the domestic needs of their families,
began finding themselves with more time and energy. At the same
time, girls were getting better opportunities for education, which
they took up enthusiastically.

With the decline of faith in the general population, convent life,
formerly a viable option for lively, intelligent and active young
women, has faded in popularity during this century. In earlier
times, nuns played a vital role in the medical and educational
fields, using their talents to provide superb care for the young and
the sick. This faithful dedication to others has proved to be irre-
placeable, though it is still alive and well in some religious orders,
such as that of Mother Teresa of India.

With the demise of full-time housework, the entry of women
into paid work and access to higher education, the modern feminist movement was born, justly demanding equal rights and opportunities for women. The movement gained a lot of sympathy in its
early days, though it also engendered great hostility.

It is interesting to see how women have been viewed throughout history. Plato, a progressive thinker who lived in Greece during
the fifth century B.C., believed that women had the talents for political, military and intellectual leadership. But Aristotle, a pupil of
Plato's, believed that women were inferior to men. Mary Woll-
stonecroft, who lived during the nineteenth century, was the first
female philosopher to address feminism. She wanted women to
live virtuously but to receive a thorough ethical training that would
allow them to become respected by men and treated as equal. John
Stuart Mill, another English philosopher of the nineteenth century,
argued that women should be allowed and encouraged to exercise
their intellectual and creative gifts as well as their maternal ones.
Among famous twentieth-century writers on feminism is Simone

de Beauvoir, a Frenchwoman. Some of her ideas have been influential in the gradual shift into radical feminism, a strand of feminism of the late twentieth century now diminishing in influence but still capable of influencing the social discourse of our times.

## Radical Feminism

Twentieth-century feminism has ranged from moderate to radical in outlook. While moderate feminism calls for no more than fair treatment for women, especially in matters such as educational opportunity and the vote, radical feminism has gone much farther. Traditionally, women's lives centered around their families. But radical feminists want to diminish the importance of the family and to extricate women from their traditional position at the heart of the family. They argue that the family institution oppresses women by keeping them subjugated and at the beck and call of men and that it denies women opportunities for self-fulfillment. As we are living in a period of social disintegration (with more divorces, more suicides, more unemployment and more homelessness), it is valid to ask whether radical feminist social policies have contributed to this breakdown.

The aims of radical feminists are indicative of their overall philosophy. They include abortion on demand, easy access to divorce, twenty-four-hour child-care centers and ready access to contraception. Not too much thought is needed to work out what these aims are meant to achieve. They represent an attack on the role of women as an integral part of the family. They are designed to relieve women of family responsibilities by encouraging work-force participation at the expense of full-time motherhood and child-raising.

Radical feminism tells women that their babies are well cared for in child-care centers and that there is no need for mothers to stay at home with their young children. It suggests that becoming a mother is less fulfilling than other life-style choices. It puts forward the idea of single parenthood, arguing that fathers are an optional extra. It facilitates women divorcing their husbands rather than finding ways of reconciliation. There are some extreme groups (sometimes found on university campuses) that espouse lesbianism.

## The Female Sexual Revolution

One of the most important beliefs of radical feminists relates to sexuality. Equality for women means for some the liberation from traditional restrictions on sexual behavior. The arrival of the contraceptive pill naturally helped this cause by removing the fear of unwanted pregnancies. Christianity has always taught that sexual intercourse, in God's plan, is to be part of marriage and moreover that it is intimately connected with having children. The sexual revolution of the 1960s and 1970s overturned this idea. The "Women's Lib" movement extolled a hedonistic idea that unfettered sex is the essence of being a free woman.

However, some feminist theory has since diversified from this stance. For example, the Australian feminist Germaine Greer, who rose to prominence during the 1970s, now sees that some of the things that "Women's Lib" feminists campaigned for have not been in the interests of women at all. She points out that contraception has some potentially severe medical side effects and that abortion can sometimes leave women not only with medical problems but also with grief and guilt. She now admits that much of what radical feminism campaigned for in the 1970s was more in the interests of unscrupulous men (and of course multinational pharmaceutical companies).

The sexual license that Western women have been encouraged to adopt is not in their interests. The psychologist Alfred Adler says that women generally want to feel valued for themselves, not just for their sexuality. It is more common for men to look for a purely sexual relationship without emotional ties. When a relationship breaks up, the woman (who may have been more committed than her partner to the union) may feel betrayed. Many women see sex as an expression of love and involvement. As a result, they are more likely than men to feel shortchanged by a society that allows sexual freedom but does not encourage sexual commitment. Increases in the divorce rate, drug taking, eating disorders, gambling, depression and loneliness are indicators that women are stressed rather than liberated by their relatively new sexual freedom.

The huge pressures in today's society to be part of the sexual revolution are coming in large part from people who have much to gain. The media have been and will continue to be influential. The pharmaceutical companies make untold millions from contraceptive devices. (There is research that shows a reliable link between the contraceptive pill and a rise in the incidence of breast cancer, strokes and vascular problems. But the findings have been all but suppressed by the multinational pharmaceutical companies.) It is most unfortunate that young people, who are least able to identify and evaluate the dangers of sexual liberty, are overwhelmingly subjected to information that works on their vulnerabilities.

## Male and Female Differences

Men and women, made by God our Creator, are profoundly different and yet complementary. As research continues into the differences between men and women, it becomes increasingly clear that these variations are not only physical but biological, psychological, emotional and even spiritual. Some of these differences are innate; others are the result of social conditioning.

Men are generally physically stronger than women and have more muscle tissue. Most men are taller and heavier than women. Women tend to live longer and are physically healthier than men. A higher proportion of males than females are more susceptible to disease and birth defects. Girls usually mature physically and emotionally at an earlier age than boys. It seems that male and female brains are "wired" differently. As science discovers more about the functions of the human brain, some fascinating facts are emerging. Scientists have found that the left hemisphere of the brain, which specializes in mathematical thinking, spatial relations and visual tasks, is generally more developed in males than in females. But more females tend to have a better developed right side of the brain, which gives them a higher degree of sensitivity and better verbal skills. Of course, there are many women who are brilliant scientists just as there are many men who have excellent verbal skills. Females are generally more diplomatic and sensitive than males in dealing with others, and women are considered to be better nurturers. One psychologist named Eric Eriksen pointed out that small boys' play often involves exterior mobility, while small girls' play often involves making shelters, pretend houses, playing with dolls and wrapping things up.

## Females and Males as Seen by Catholics

Many thinkers, including Saint Augustine, Saint Thomas Aquinas and Pope John Paul II, have insisted that although men and women are different, they are equal in their fundamental relationships. This is because they have been created for each other, which in turn is also why the male/female relationship is the most satisfactory and successful one.

Pope John Paul's ideas are worth examining. As Bishop Karol Wojtyla, he wrote a book called *Love and Responsibility*, in which he said: "A woman wants to be loved so that she can show love; a man wants to love so that he can be loved." For a man who has never been married, the Pope shows an extraordinary insight into marriage. He also wrote that "the woman feels her role in marriage is to give herself. The man's experience is different: its psychological correlative is possession." And again: "A woman is only capable of making herself a gift if she believes in her value as a person and in the value of the man to whom she gives herself."

## Parenthood and the Future of Women

Motherhood is one of the richest of all human experiences, and it engenders some of the best characteristics, such as courage, intelligence, ingenuity, gentleness, tenderness, generosity and unselfishness. The bond between a mother and her child is considered by many to be the closest of all human bonds. This is easy to understand when we consider that for the first nine months of a baby's life, it is nurtured within its mother's body.

The way ahead for parents will be challenging, as some roles are redefined and others are reinforced. The future should see a time of reconciliation, a time when more men and women learn to treat each other with justice and respect. For both women and men, parenthood will continue to be an exercise in balancing private and professional priorities. While women have an enormous range of talents that are of inestimable value in the paid workforce and public affairs, only they can be the wives of husbands and the mothers of children. These experiences are too valuable to be given away lightly or to be treated as of only secondary importance.

Perhaps it is time for a new expression of the feminine—but this can only be achieved with a similarly new expression of the position of men in our society. Women and men are truly made for each other, and only together can they grow into the likeness of God, procreate descendants and hold dominion over the earth.

## Bibliography

*Catechism of the Catholic Church*, pt. 1, sec. 2, chap. 1, art. 1, pars. 369–73.

The following sources were used to review some of the issues relating to feminism:

Gilder, George, *Men and Marriage*, chap. 2 (Pelican Publishers, 1986), for the biological differences between men and women.

Stein, Edith, *Essays on Woman*, chap. 11 (Washington, D.C.: ICS Books, 1987).

Wojtyla, Karol, *Love and Responsibility* (New York: Farrar, Straus & Giroux, 1981).

*For Review*

1. Explain how Mary may be seen as a perfect model for women.

2. What is meant by the term "sexual revolution"? What outcomes have we seen as a result of the sexual revolution?

3. Explain how men and women can be said to complement each other.

• • • • • • • • • • • • • • • • • • • • • • • •

*Consider These*

1. Should women who stay at home with their babies be specially honored? Why/why not?

2. At the Beijing Conference on Women in 1995, Mother Teresa said: "I do not understand why some people . . . are denying the beautiful differences between men and women. . . . Together they show God's love more fully than either could do alone. . . . We can destroy this gift of motherhood . . . No job, no plans, no possessions, no idea of 'freedom' can take the place of love." What do you think of this statement?

3. Think of several female icons of the present day such as the singer Madonna, Diana the Princess of Wales and the actor Nicole Kidman. What is it about them that has made them interesting to the media? Do the media reflect the interests and concerns of their consumers, or do they generate their own ideals and interests?

4. In what ways can women's attitudes toward men reinforce the best that men are capable of?

*Extension Exercises*

1. Talk to someone of your own generation and find out what being female means to him. Then ask the same question of someone of your parents' and grandparents' generations. What differences do you find? What about men's attitudes toward women? Do they appear to have changed between generations?

2. Examine some of the magnificent works of art from the Renaissance period, especially the various studies of the Madonna and Child. Why was this subject such a preoccupation with Renaissance artists? Why is it not so now?

3. Watch the movie *My Brilliant Career*, which is based on a book by Australian novelist Miles Franklin (pseudonym of Stella Maria Sarah Miles Franklin). What does the movie suggest about the situation of Australian women during the 1800s?

# CHAPTER TWELVE

# Euthanasia: Is Killing Kind?

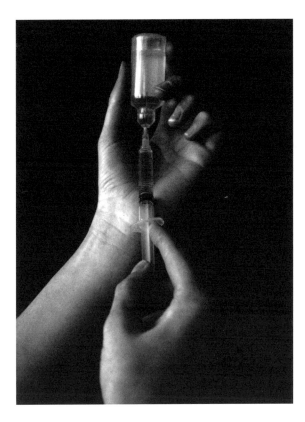

*Why is euthanasia a threat?*

These days, euthanasia is a much-discussed topic. It usually evokes strong feelings of support or opposition. But what exactly is euthanasia? How do the teachings of the Church help us to understand the moral problems involved?

## What Is Euthanasia?

For the ancient Greeks, euthanasia meant an easy death without severe suffering. Today, there is much confusion and controversy over dying with dignity, allowing people to die, the necessity of prolonging life and euthanasia itself. To begin unravelling this confusion, we should realize that euthanasia has a precise meaning: it is an action or an omitted action that causes death so that suffering is eliminated. Usually motivated by compassion, it is the deliberate termination of the life of someone afflicted with an incurable and progressive disease or of someone whose life is considered not worth living. By definition, euthanasia is final. There is no second chance, no possibility of changing one's mind. Another name for euthanasia is mercy killing.

Euthanasia is voluntary when performed with the consent of the dying person. But sometimes a patient, for example, a severely disabled infant or a person in a coma, may not be capable of consenting and never requests euthanasia. The termination of the life of such a person is called nonvoluntary euthanasia. In no country is nonvoluntary euthanasia legal, although voluntary euthanasia has gained support within a number of countries.

Sometimes people distinguish "active" euthanasia (performing an action such as giving an injection to cause death) from "passive" euthanasia (deliberately withholding treatment or support). In both situations, the same effect is intended, namely, the death of the sufferer.

Euthanasia is different from suicide. Euthanasia involves the killing of one person (a patient) by another (often a doctor), whereas suicide is the intentional killing of oneself. Assisting a suicide means providing help to someone to kill himself.

## Sanctity of Life

Christians regard life as wonderful and sacred, the high point of all creation and the supreme expression of God's love. As we are custodians, not owners, of the life God has given us, we are obliged to respect and preserve human life from the moment of conception. It is therefore a crime, a violation of a basic human right, to attempt to kill an innocent person. We also have an obligation to God, who is the master of life, to preserve our own lives. Human life is not ours to give away. Therefore suicide, euthanasia and any other form of murder is wrong.

The ability to choose freely and knowingly distinguishes humans from animals. But God gave us our freedom to choose good, not evil. Suicide is a sin against oneself and a violation of self-respect. It also selfishly breaks the ties of solidarity with society, friends and family. However, we should distinguish suicide from sacrificing one's life for a higher cause, as in the just defense of one's country or in the upholding of one's faith even in the face of death.

## Dignity in Death

"Dying with dignity" means entirely different things to different people. The term has been adopted by various organizations as a slogan to promote the cause of voluntary euthanasia and assisted suicide. Some extreme groups even see it as a slogan to encourage legal protection for the nonvoluntary euthanasia of certain categories of persons, such as those who are mentally disabled. True death with dignity is the process of helping a dying patient by providing as much physical relief and emotional support as possible. Treatment that is of no further benefit to the patient can be withdrawn.

In many cases, proper relief of a dying person's pain can prolong the patient's life as stress is relieved. There is much ignorance about the ability of experienced doctors to relieve pain. The provision of adequate relief can allow many terminally ill patients to live longer and to die in greater peace. Doctors have an obligation to use every reasonable means to free patients from pain and suffering. Intense suffering so dominates consciousness that many patients find that personally important activities become almost impossible to undertake. The relief of such pain is not designed to terminate life, even if this is a possible consequence, but to liberate, to enable the sick to speak to their loved ones, perhaps to pray and to be at peace.

In the course of every illness, the time arrives when it is no longer possible to reverse the dying process. Prolonging a person's

death, perhaps through the use of sophisticated technology and at
the cost of great suffering, is not the right thing to do. It is appropriate to allow these people to die while doing what we can to
bring peace and eliminate pain.

## Discontinuing Treatment

Saving lives has always been the central goal of medical practice.
However, doctors also have a professional obligation to respect the
independence and dignity of each patient. When is it permissible,
then, to discontinue treatment, even though the death of the
patient is foreseen?

Doctors should not insist on a particular treatment against the
informed, free and stable refusal of a nonsuicidal patient who is
well enough to make such a decision, i.e., not brainwashed or
pathologically depressed.

Life-prolonging treatments are not likely to be appropriate
when they cause more suffering than benefit. Neither are patients
obliged to undergo treatments that are futile, such as some chemo-
therapies, which may have a very low probability of success, or
where a particular treatment might be successful but the patient's
underlying condition is catastrophic for another reason. A patient
can refuse "overzealous" treatment where the medical procedures
are burdensome, dangerous, extraordinary or disproportionate to
the expected outcome. In such a case, neither patient nor doctor
decides to cause death; rather, both concede that they are unable
to impede dying.

Such decisions are best made by the patients themselves, or by
their agents or family if they are incapable of choosing the course
of action, in consultation with medical staff. All involved must
always respect the reasonable decisions and legitimate interests
of the patient.

## Care and Treatment

We always have an obligation to provide appropriate care for the
sick and dying, although such care takes different forms in differ-

ent situations. Basic care means making patients comfortable and implies providing essentials such as food, water, bedrest, a comfortable room temperature, and personal hygiene. Giving food to the hungry and water to the thirsty is a requirement of elementary human decency. The mechanical delivery of food and fluids can, in unusual circumstances, by exception, qualify as "extraordinary means" and thus be ethically optional. When a patient is near the time of to death, providing fluids could cause discomfort, and food may not be digested as the body begins "shutting down". When inevitable death is truly imminent (within twenty-four to forty-eight hours), a simple wiping of the brow and moistening of the lips with ice may be all that is appropriate. We are not entitled to abandon people simply because they are a burden to us and society.

People with a serious illness or incapacity have as much right to live as those who are well. We have to continue to care for and feed the disabled, the demented, the abandoned and the unwanted. Removing food and water because a person is considered burdensome or "better off dead" is a way of killing that person, directly, intentionally and cruelly. Killing must never become an accepted medical treatment. Giving drugs to relieve pain is acceptable, even when it is foreseen that providing some narcotics may shorten life or bring about unconsciousness.

## The Relief of Suffering

We kill animals when they are suffering to put them out of their misery. Humans are more than animals. Each of us has a unique dignity, a right to receive respect from others, no matter what our condition. All people have the right to live with serious illness or incapacity. No one has a right to be killed, just as we have no right to maim ourselves.

Because we do not kill suffering humans, we do have a solemn obligation to bring relief. Due to the spectacular advances in palliative care (which relieves pain and suffering but does not cure illness), we are able to provide relief to sufferers much better than in the past. Good palliative care helps family and friends as well as the patient. However, we should not claim that pain can always be eliminated completely. Illness can still bring heavy suffering in about 2 to 5 percent of cases.

Patients generally have confidence in the good intentions of doctors and nurses because of the premises on which our health system is based. But unfortunately, this confidence is fraying at the edges. Some expectant mothers carefully choose the hospital where they give birth because they are fearful of the fate of their babies if born imperfect. (Writer Peter Carey's 1994 novel *The Unusual Life of Tristan Smith* explores this theme.)

If voluntary euthanasia were to be made legally or practically available, such unease would spread into new areas. For example, family pressures, some inspired by genuine concern, some by selfishness and unscrupulousness, would be exerted on the elderly to encourage them to take a quick exit or to end their lives quietly. The fears of the old and infirm would increase.

In short, the legalization of voluntary euthanasia, even under strict guidelines, is wrong because even with the best of intentions it leads to murder or suicide, both forbidden by God's law. The principle of universal care would be eroded, and it would become more difficult for our society to remain caring and altruistic, especially as the financial pressures on the health dollar would continue to be formidable. Euthanasia would certainly reduce health costs and will continue to be a temptation to those who consider finance the first priority. The dangers from such financial pressures are another reason to continue our uncompromising stand against a law permitting the administration of death.

Until the final day of judgment, the sun will continue to rise on the just and the unjust. Laws, therefore, must protect and restrain people of ill will as well as the pure of heart. We do not live in an ideal world.

## Experiments with Euthanasia This Century

In 1920, a lawyer named Karl Binding and a doctor named Alfred Hoche published a book in Germany advocating euthanasia. They did not foresee that their ideas on mercy killing would be taken so much farther by the Nazis in their vile attempts to "purify" the gene pool. But the postwar Nuremberg trials of Nazi war criminals have shown that their book influenced the Nazi programmers. This terrible historical development reminds us not to be naive about the long-term consequences of decriminalizing euthanasia.

The most infamous society for euthanasia today is Holland. Although euthanasia remains technically illegal, cases are not prosecuted provided they are carried out with certain precautions and procedures, for example, the doctor must provide a written report explaining and justifying his actions. In September 1991, a committee of enquiry sponsored by the Dutch Government issued the Remmelink Report entitled *Euthanasia and Other Medical Decisions concerning the End of Life*. By using the Remmelink data and basing calculations on a total annual mortality rate of 129,000, the Dutch Physicians League estimated that doctors intended (implicitly or explicitly) to end the lives of 20,000 patients, which made up 15 percent of all deaths. In such societies where killing is a regular method of problem solving, which of us is safe?

## Euthanasia and Law

The legal situation differs from country to country. Indeed, there is some confusion about what the different laws actually allow. One source of this confusion is the contrasting obligations of doctors who are expected, on the one hand, to preserve life and take reasonable care of their patients and, on the other hand, not to trespass illegally against the wishes of their patients. Euthanasia is occurring in an unknown number of cases. The legal situation is imperfect and changing; nevertheless, the practical problems would not be lessened nor the legal problems clarified by legalizing euthanasia.

## Christians on Death and Suffering

Christians believe that all those who die in God's friendship enter heaven, a state of supreme definitive happiness, and enjoy perfect life with the Holy Trinity. Scripture uses images such as the wedding feast, light and peace to point to the nature of this blessed communion with God, but the nature of heaven is beyond our knowledge and imagination.

There is a similar difference between believers and unbelievers in their understanding of pain and suffering. For those who do not believe in God, pain is a brute fact, only sometimes biologically useful as a warning of illness. Christians also fight against suffering, but we believe that Christ has redeemed us through his suffering and death. In some mysterious way, pain accepted in faith can be turned to good.

Christians are encouraged to unite their personal sufferings with those of Christ and thereby participate in the saving work of Jesus. We are taught to offer our sufferings to God for particular purposes, such as to stop a war or for worthy causes or for the well-being of loved ones.

• • • • • • • • • • • • • • • • • • • • • • • • •

*Bibliography*

*Catechism of the Catholic Church*, pt. 3, sec. 2, chap. 2, art. 5, pars. 2258–83.

## For Review

1. Is euthanasia more than "dying with dignity"? How do you define it?

2. Why is there no right to die?

3. What is meant by a "good death"?

## Consider These

1. Why is palliative care important? What will happen to the development of palliative care if euthanasia is introduced?

2. "The demand for euthanasia comes not from sick or old people but from their families." How true is this claim?

3. Explain why the Catholic Church always allows measures to eliminate or control pain and suffering.

4. Can human existence ever be pointless and meaningless?

5. "If laws permitting euthanasia are introduced, the most vulnerable will be the very young, the feeble and marginalized people." Is this a reasonable claim?

6. "The most important difference between religious and pagan people today is found in their attitudes toward suffering." Is this true? What is the difference?

## Extension Exercises

1. *April Fool's Day*, a book by Bryce Courtenay, tells the story of the author's young hemophiliac son who was killed by the AIDS

virus received from a blood transfusion. Would you be more or less likely to recommend euthanasia for your son than for a stranger? Why/why not?

2. Euthanasia, like suicide, is an expression of despair. This mood is well caught in the (AIDS) Symphony No. 1, written by the contemporary American composer John Corigliano, especially with the tolling bell of the final movement. In your experience, is it true that strong religious faith protects people from despair? yes.

3. Listen to the second movement of Beethoven's famous "Eroica" (Third) Symphony, which Beethoven described as the funeral march for a great leader. What feelings does this music express? Why is euthanasia incompatible with the grandeur of the human spirit?

4. Examine the issues behind some of the legal battles over euthanasia.

# CHAPTER THIRTEEN

# What's Wrong with Abortion?

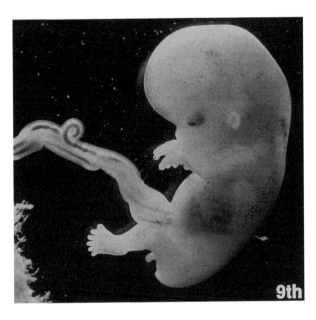

*A nine-week-old human fetus. What are the rights of an unborn child?*

Abortion was legalized in the English-speaking world in the late 1960s and early 1970s. However, Catholics and many other Christians have never believed that abortions are morally right. Therefore, opinions are strongly divided. It is important to understand the Christian side of the argument.

Abortion is the termination of a pregnancy before birth. Early spontaneous or natural abortions are usually described as miscarriages, while the term "abortion" implies a deliberate human act.

Induced abortions have been regarded as an offense in most civilizations, and the Church has always taught that abortion is gravely wrong. The Greek physician Hippocrates of Cos (who died around 377 B.C.) is often described as the author of the Hippocratic oath, which explains the obligations of doctors. However, the earliest versions of this oath come from before the sixth century B.C. Certainly the oath shows that the prohibition of abortion is pre-Christian in origin: "I will neither give a deadly drug to anybody if asked for it, nor will I make a suggestion to this effect. Similarly I will not give a woman an abortive remedy." The early second-century instruction called the *Didache* (or *Teaching of the Twelve Apostles*) taught, "You shall not kill the embryo by abortion or cause the newborn to perish" (2.2).

The Church's teaching on this matter has not changed through the centuries and, indeed, cannot be changed, because it is a fundamental part of God's law that the Church must defend. The Scriptures themselves never speak of intentional abortion, but the many beautiful passages on childbirth and unborn children reveal Scripture as radically pro-life and profoundly sympathetic to expectant mothers.

In the Old and New Testaments, both the conception and formation of children in the womb are portrayed as the work of God (Psalm 139:13–15; Luke 1:35). For example, the Christmas story has many layers of symbolism.

The Christian teaching against abortion links the scriptural teaching on the sanctity of the unborn with the explicit Old Testament and New Testament teachings against killing the innocent. In the Sermon on the Mount, our Lord recalls the commandment "You shall not kill" and adds to it the proscription of anger, hatred and vengeance (Matthew 5:21; Exodus 20:13).

### Beginnings

The word "embryo" refers to human offspring in the first eight weeks from conception. "Fetus" refers to an unborn child more than eight weeks old. The human characteristics of an embryo and fetus are crucial to explaining the pro-life case against abortion. The Catholic Church teaches that from the moment of conception, the egg fertilized by the sperm must be treated as a human being and accorded the respect due to a person. Advances in genetic knowledge over the last fifty to one hundred years have strengthened this conviction.

Originally, many Church teachers distinguished between a formed and unformed fetus, claiming that the soul was not infused at conception. The greatest theologian of the early Church, Saint Augustine of North Africa, who died in A.D. 430, believed that the embryo was ensouled at forty-six days. Nevertheless, he also believed that it was gravely wrong to kill a formed or unformed fetus. Another great Catholic thinker, the Italian Saint Thomas Aquinas, who died in 1274, believed ensoulment took place forty days after conception for the male and at ninety days after conception for the female.

Through the advances of modern microbiology, we now know better. One hour after the sperm has penetrated the ovum, the nuclei of the two cells have already fused. From that moment, there is a set of genetic instructions to establish the code or inheritance for the new person. After seven or eight days, this ball of cells travels down the Fallopian tube to reach the womb, where it implants. The child then releases hormones into the mother so that her body begins to supply it with nutrients.

By twenty-five days, the embryo's developing heart starts beating. By thirty-three days, the embryo is about 2.8 inches long and has also developed a brain, eyes, ears, mouth, kidneys, liver, umbilical cord and a heart pumping blood that it is producing. By forty-five days, about the time of the mother's second missed period, the embryo's skeleton is complete (in cartilage, not bone), and the first movements of limb and body occur. By ten weeks, the fetus can grasp an object placed in its palm and clench its fist, and it can respond to pain, touch, cold, sound and light. It wakes and sleeps, gets the hiccups and can suck its thumb. It can be seen that the fetus has a life independent of its mother, and, although dependent on her for survival, its life is not identical with hers.

## Reasons for Abortion

The United States, United Kingdom, Australia and New Zealand often follow similar patterns in moral, legal and political matters.

Until the Second World War, the public consensus was strongly against abortion, although most British-based legal systems allowed abortion to preserve the mother's physical and mental health after the 1938 case *R v. Bourne* in the U.K.

Long-term, well-planned campaigns to enlarge the right to abortion started to have impact when the *Abortion Act* of 1967 was passed in England. The new legislation made it possible to have an abortion if it could be argued that the birth would lead to mental and physical health risks to any of the existing family, or if physical or mental abnormalities were likely to exist in the child. In 1973, the Supreme Court of the United States in the *Roe v. Wade* case ruled that a constitutional right to privacy included the right to have an abortion at any time until the twenty-sixth week of pregnancy. (However, determined legal and political efforts are now being made in the U.S. to change or restrict the practical effects of this ruling, and "Jane Roe" [the plaintiff in the case] is now pro-life because she has come to realize what was being destroyed.)

In the late 1960s in places such as South Australia and the United Kingdom, psychiatric illness was alleged as the reason for abortion in 80 percent of cases. Today, few people feel it is necessary to claim mental illness in order to be allowed to have an abortion. Unfortunately, some abortions take place because of the cost and distress another child will bring (even in prosperous countries), because of the diagnosis of fetal abnormalities, and even for reasons of convenience. The desire for perfect children can be like issuing a death warrant for babies with abnormalities, real or possible.

The right to abortion has become an important symbol for radical feminists, who often see it as an essential dimension of a woman's right to control her own body and a necessary expression of personal autonomy and individual freedom. They call their approach "pro-choice". But there is a terrible cost to unborn babies. This stance also ignores the fact that women themselves can be harmed by abortion, many living with grief or guilt for the rest of their lives. The pro-choice slogan refers only to the mother—there is no choice for the unborn child.

The Church forbids the destruction of all innocent life, there-fore, she also condemns the direct killing of a fetus, even to safe-guard the life of the mother. However, the Church does not forbid the unavoidable death of a fetus directly occasioned by a surgical operation necessarily performed for another purpose, for example, the removal of a cancerous uterus or of a Fallopian tube containing an ectopic pregnancy.

Here the Church is using a line of moral argument called the principle of double effect. The principle states that a good effect can be achieved properly even when other incidental but unavoid-able harm is caused, as when manufacturers produce motor cars so that people can travel quickly even though it is foreseen that cars will be involved in traffic accidents causing deaths.

## Abortion Methods

During the first twelve to fourteen weeks of pregnancy, abortion is usually performed by forceps removal or suction curettage. In this procedure, the baby is actually dismembered, torn limb from limb. At the next stage of fourteen to twenty weeks, injections of hyper-tonic glucose or saline into the fetus' amniotic sac are the lethal agents. The fetus is literally pickled to death, and this process takes about an hour or longer. At twenty to twenty-eight weeks, dismembering or even hysterotomy is used, similar to a Caesarean operation. This is particularly barbaric and dangerous for the mother and has recently been outlawed in Japan because of the side effects.

The IUD (intrauterine device), which is inserted into the uterus as a means of birth control, usually causes abortions because it is thought to interfere with implantation of the embryo. The IUD can cause serious health complications, especially for women who want to bear children in the future. Indeed, 200,000 women have filed lawsuits against the producers of Dalkon Shield, an early IUD, alleging severe adverse effects.

Another method of abortion, that many people do not recog-nize, is caused by "The Pill". There are many varieties of the birth control pill, but most of them have the same basic functions. The primary way in which the pill works is to stop ovulation. If there is no egg being ovulated, conception cannot occur. This is often not effective, so the pill has several other functions to inhibit pregnancy. The basic action of the pill is to inhibit the sperm and the egg from ever meeting. But, if that does occur, there is one last effect. The pill works to alter the endometrial lining of the uterus so that the fertilized egg can not implant. The developing embryo is allowed to be sloughed off, which is an early abortion. A woman who regularly uses the pill can have a number of abortions a year without even knowing that she has conceived.

The drug RU-486, also known as the abortion pill, causes abortions without surgery. It has been tested to produce abortions in the first seven weeks of pregnancy. The Food and Drug Administration approved this drug in 1996 for use in the United States. It, like many drugs, has serious side effects and can cause liver damage, heart damage, or sterility.

## Sanctity of Human Life

A few philosophers, such as Peter Singer and Helga Kuhse, have started to teach that human life is not sacred and imply that human beings are only a higher form of animal. In an article published in the *Spectator* in 1995, Singer wrote:

> Yes, we can say, the foetus is a living human being, but that alone is not sufficient to show that it is wrong to end its life. After all, why . . . should mere membership of the species *Homo sapiens* be crucial to whether the life of a being may or may not be taken? Surely what is important is the capacities or characteristics that a being has. It is doubtful if a foetus becomes conscious until quite late in pregnancy, well after the time at which abortions are usually performed; and even the presence of consciousness would put a foetus at a level comparable to a rather simple non-human animal—not that of a dog, let alone a chimpanzee.

Modern Western civilization, religious and irreligious, gives the lie to this nonsense. Medical research demonstrates that the fetus reacts to pain at ten weeks. Ask the mother of any newborn child, even if the child be sick or dying, physically or psychologically handicapped, and she will tell you that her child is worth more than one million animals and that it differs from any animal more than cheese differs from chalk, and therefore has the right to live. Every human being, even if unable to speak, smile, pray or curse, is made in God's image and destined for eternal life. This religious truth is based on the huge differences between self-conscious humans, who are capable of thinking, and brute animals.

The almost universal conviction about the importance of every human life is the bedrock of the Western world's politics, law and daily living. This is why many governments require that each child be educated, why all adults have a right to vote, why the United Nations has a charter of universal human rights, why we are horrified by child abuse, why we donate money to help the victims of violence and famine, and why many oppose capital punishment, even for murderers. But unfortunately, in practice this principle is not always respected as it should be. Even then, those driven by sin and self-interest usually prefer to jostle the principle, to circumvent or reinterpret it, rather than to deny or remove it completely.

The supporters of abortion often deny that the unborn child is new human life, calling it part of the mother's body. They also often oppose any proposals to show films or photos of their destructive work; of the baby's skull being pierced or crushed; of the tiny body disintegrating under powerful suction.

Society must not lapse back to barbaric times, such as the period of the pre-Christian Roman Empire, when slavery and infanticide were practiced. In mainland China today, the government's "one family, one child" policy means that millions of babies, especially girls, are aborted, killed as infants or placed in orphanages. There is already a severe imbalance in the number of men and women as a result of this policy.

The conviction that human life is sacred means that nowhere should abortion or infanticide be condoned, even when it is practiced in secret or on deformed and retarded children.

**Health Risks**

In the 1960s, when there was much more public discussion about the immorality (or permissibility) of abortion, one of the frequently stated ambitions of the abortion lobby was to diminish the number of maternal deaths and injuries brought about by "backyard" abortionists. Often, this morbidity rate was exaggerated.

A different veil of silence now covers the medical risks to the mother from legalized abortions under good medical conditions. Induced abortions are neither safe nor simple. There is hard evidence of unfortunate medical sequels to abortion, especially in subsequent childbirth—for example, an increase in premature births, ectopic pregnancies and a whole range of diseases. As well, there is the immense harm to the psyche or spiritual well-being of many of the women involved. In 1994, newspapers highlighted more than twenty research projects that had investigated the increased risk of breast cancer for women who had undergone abortions. Such research is no doubt of interest to many people because about 1,500,000 Americans each year have induced abortions with far more worldwide.

• • • • • • • • • • • • • • • • • • • • • • • •

*Bibliography*

*Catechism of the Catholic Church*, pt. 3, sec. 2, chap. 2, art. 5, pars. 2270–75.

The following sources were used to research the views of Peter Singer and Helga Kuhse:

Singer, Peter, "Killing Babies Isn't Always Wrong", *Spectator*, September 16, 1995, 20–22. Singer, Peter, *Rethinking Life and Death* (1994).

Singer, Peter, and Helga Kuhse, *Should the Baby Live?* (1985).

## For Review

1. Why does the Catholic Church reject abortion?

2. Why is human life sacred?

3. How are abortions performed?

## Consider These

1. a. Write a paragraph describing how you would support a close friend who has indicated that she is thinking of having an abortion.

   b. How would you help a friend who has had an abortion and wishes that she had not?

2. Some people say that the Church has no right to impose her view on others. In a democracy, do we have a right to oppose abortion publicly?

3. Some countries have legalized abortion but only when there is a threat to the life of the mother. What is the stance of the Church in such situations?

4. Do you think that an embryo or a fetus is a human being? What are your reasons?

## Extension Exercises

1. The following poem, entitled "The Sticking-point . . . it out Herods Herod (Hamlet)", was written by well-known poet Bruce Dawe.

I am a man, I know
—but I still say
that life is life
and death is surely death
—to kill the growing child
in any way
is to rob the future
of its breath.

The means are many,
the result's the same:
life that already is
must cease to be
—I am not reassured
that when they came
such deaths were in the name
of liberty . . .

I only know
that every year the world
solves the insoluble
at infinite cost,
that every morning petals
part-unfurled
are brought to nothing by
a killing frost . . .

a. Explain the attitude to abortion presented in this poem. Give quotations to support your statements.

b. What do you think is meant by "the world solves the insoluble at infinite cost"? Discuss how this line may be applied to a range of issues.

c. What do you think of the title of the poem?

2. Do you know a family with a disabled child? Describe the special love that is apparent in such a family. Why is this so?

# CHAPTER FOURTEEN

# How Many Children?

*Are children blessings?*
*Is the earth overpopulated?*

We have all heard of the threat of a worldwide population explosion, limited supplies of food and poverty in many countries of the Third World. How justified are these fears? How much accurate information is available? How reliable are current estimates, and how precise have predictions been during the last forty to fifty years? Does the Catholic Church have anything to say on global and national issues of this nature?

Such important public questions are essential background for some of the equally important personal decisions young adults have to make as they consider marrying and having children of their own. How many children should responsible parents have today? What means should be used to achieve their goals?

Because of their childhood experiences and the current rate of marriage breakdown, some young people are reluctant, even frightened, to marry. A smaller number also claim that they do not want to bring children into today's world. Are these responses reasonable? Are they appropriate for believing Christians?

## Malthus

The first important writer in English on the population problem was the Anglican clergyman Thomas Robert Malthus (1766–1834), who published his *Essay on Population* in 1798, when the population of the world was probably about one billion people. He believed that the population was already too large for the world's food supply and that terrible disasters were imminent because of population growth and the resulting imbalance in "the proportion between the natural increase of population and food".

His book was very influential, although it provoked a great deal of opposition, especially from the religiously minded and the general public. He did not approve of abortion or contraception, believing that only economic necessity would induce people to marry late and have fewer children. Therefore, he opposed the British Government's "poor laws", which were designed to bring relief to the poverty-stricken, because he believed that the legislation encouraged people to have too many babies!

He was followed by a group of nineteenth-century British thinkers who came to be known as the "neo-Malthusians". Jeremy Bentham and John Stuart Mill were probably the best known of them. While accepting Malthus' basic argument that overpopulation was a fact, they differed from him on contraception, believing that the poor should be taught about the necessity and methods of contraception. However, they did not teach their views publicly because they feared massive public hostility. (Before that time, there had been no public support for contraception in Christian Europe for fifteen hundred years. Public acceptance dates only from this century, when the first contraception clinic anywhere opened in London in 1921.)

• • • • • • • • • • • • • • • • • • • • • • • • • • • • • • • • • • • • •

The alarmist predictions of Malthus have not come to pass. Indeed, so far, he has been proved quite wrong. The world population is now around six billion, but people are living longer and in generally better conditions. Per capita food production and consumption are now much higher.

## Ehrlich

Perhaps the most influential contemporary "doomsday writer" on the threats to our planet is Paul Ehrlich (a biologist from Stanford University in the United States), who in 1968 published *The Population Bomb*, which sold two million copies. In 1990 he and his wife Anne published *The Population Explosion*. Three sections of the 1968 book were headed "Too Many People", "Too Little Food" and "A Dying Planet". The prologue to this book began, "The battle to feed all of humanity is over. In the 1970s the world will undergo famines—hundreds of millions are going to starve to death. . . ." Obviously, this did not happen: for the eight terrible famines throughout the world that occurred between 1968 and 1983, deaths are estimated at a little below 3,500,000, which is less than 2 percent of what Ehrlich predicted.

Ehrlich made predictions about many other topics, such as: food production; oxygen depletion (through burning fossil fuels); a baby boom in the U.S. in the 1970s; the need for water; estimates of fish production; and even the alleged destruction of Lake Erie. On all of these issues, Ehrlich has been spectacularly wrong.

In 1981 Ehrlich made a public bet with Julian Simon (the best-known opponent of population control) that five nongovernment-controlled resources of Ehrlich's choosing would increase in real price in the following ten years. Ehrlich chose copper, chrome, nickel, tin and tungsten. He was wrong in each case, with the prices decreasing by 56.7 percent on average by 1991. Ehrlich paid Simon $567. The enthusiasm for exaggeration that gained Ehrlich much publicity cannot be squared with the facts.

**World Population**

The population of the world in 1993 was about 5.5 billion people.
Thousands of years were needed to reach the first billion, then 123
years to reach the second billion, thirty-three years to reach the
third billion, fourteen years to reach the fourth billion, and thirteen
years to reach the fifth billion. Between 1980 and 1990, the world's
population grew by about 923 million.

Ninety percent of this increase took place in the developing
world, much of it in Asia, where there was an increase of 517 million people, including 146 million in China and 166 million in
India. However, the growth rate has been declining over the past
three decades: there was a 2.2 percent growth rate between 1970
and 1980, but only a 1.7 percent growth rate between 1980 and
1992. Most demographers expect this trend to continue until the
world's population becomes more or less stable.

To keep a population stable, 2.1 children per woman are
needed. In 1993, the European average (excluding Russia) was 1.6
children per woman, and in some countries, such as Greece, Italy
and Spain, the rate was around 1.3. The birthrate per woman in
the Italian city of Bologna is 0.9. Unless there are changes in practice, probably as a result of government policies encouraging families and children, commentators see the population of Europe
declining by tens of millions in the next fifty years.

The United Nations has taken upon itself the responsibility of
regulating the population of the world. They held a world conference on population in Cairo in 1994 with the intention of discussing strategies for limiting population growth around the world.
The goal of the proposals was to stabilize the world's population
at 7.27 billion by the year 2000. The population of the world at the
time of the conference was approximately 5.67 billion and the estimated population at the year 2000, without these proposed con-
trols, would be 12.5 billion.

While many of the goals of the United Nations at this conference and the world conference on the role of women that took
place in Beijing in 1995 are laudable, the Vatican has been in strict
opposition with many of the propositions at both of these events.
The discussion at these conferences has centered mainly around

the treatment of women in various countries. There are still many countries around the world that do not recognize the rights of women and treat them as lesser citizens. The Catholic Church endorses many of the UN proposals including the statement of the family as the basic unit of society and the encouragement of gender equality. What the Church does not agree with are the methods of gender equality that the United Nations proposes. They say that women cannot be equal to men without using artificial contraception and having access to abortion. They hope to make these services a part of regular health care. The Vatican is joined by many Muslim and Latin American countries who see these as direct violations of their religious beliefs.

The Catholic position on population growth is that it is not a hindrance to development in itself. There are many other hindrances to development such as education, nutrition, medicine, agriculture, economics and politics which must be improved in order to better the situation of these developing countries. The Church recognizes the importance of this development based on the dignity of each individual person. Because all people are made in God's image and have personal dignity, it is a human obligation to assist in improving the lives of as many people as possible. Because of this, the Catholic Church works together with other organizations throughout the world in charitable causes whenever these projects do not compromise the morals of Catholics.

**Population Estimates**

Many countries do not have an efficient census. Therefore, a lot of population statistics are estimates only and of differing reliability rather than certainties. Nigeria, the tenth most populated country in the world, is one example: the official 1991 Nigerian government census, which used 800,000 staff as enumerators, gave a census total of 88.5 million; whereas the United Nations Population Fund estimated Nigeria's population in 1990 to be 117 million.

Examining the overall growth in world population figures is of only limited use because of enormous regional differences. The large increase in the world's population has occurred mainly in the

Third World (especially in Asia), while the population of Europe is in decline. The birth rate in Italy is now 1.21, the lowest in the world. (Just to replace the population, without any growth, the birth rate needs to be 2.1). Rather than worrying about too many people, Italy is having problems finding enough people to work to keep the economy stable. Should population pressures in China mean that the rest of the world should be forced to have fewer children?

The increase in the world's population this century is not so much the result of increased fertility, which also varies in different countries, but rather of a decline in mortality rates. People are living longer because of better food, medicine and education. These are blessings and provide reasons for gratitude rather than for lamenting.

We should also realize that countries with high population densities are not necessarily poor. Hong Kong has the highest population density of any country, with 5,880 inhabitants per square kilometer (.3861 square mile), and Singapore has the second highest, with 4,540 inhabitants per square kilometer. Japan has a population density of 331 inhabitants per square kilometer, and the United States has 28.2 inhabitants per square kilometer. Australia has only 2.3 inhabitants per square kilometer.

Few people and plenty of land do not automatically guarantee prosperity either. Most of the countries of sub-Saharan Africa, except Rwanda, but especially some of the countries with the worst poverty problems, such as Chad, Sudan and Ethiopia, are not heavily populated at all. Poverty and famine can also be caused by wars and genocidal strife, as in Cambodia under Pol Pot and more recently in Rwanda and Bosnia.

This can be seen in the declining birth rates of some developing countries. In Colombia in the past thirty years, the fertility rate has dropped from 7.1 children for each woman to 2.9. And in Thailand in the same time, the fertility rate has been reduced from 6.5 to 2.1 children per woman. This drop in the fertility rate does not guarantee economic success since these countries are still suffering from poverty.

The total fertility rate in North America in 1989 was 1.85. This

• • • • • • • • • • • • • • • • • • • • • • • • • • • • • • • • • • • • •

is significantly below the 2.1 needed to replace the population. The increase in the population of the United States is due in large part to immigration. In 1988, 643,000 immigrants came into the United States adding to the U.S. population for that year of 246 million. The standard of living of the United States, and all western countries, is steadily increasing. In 1989, the average lifetime in the U.S. was 75.6 years and, due to continual medical and scientific advances, this figure is constantly rising.

## Pollution

Educated opinion in the Western world is now well aware of the dangers of many forms of pollution, and much progress has been made in cleaning up the atmosphere and waterways, reducing dangerous gas emissions and limiting the damage to humans from industrial waste. We should remember, however, that the worst pollution comes from industrial development and high rates of consumption rather than from the simple fact of human population.

One estimate at the 1992 Rio Earth Summit was that if all the population of the Third World were eliminated (85 percent of the earth's population), environmental degradation would only be reduced by 10 percent. The Third World has as much right (and need) as the First World to industrial development. It would, indeed, be a new form of "white colonialism" to oppose industrial development in the Third World under the guise of a simple-minded environmentalism. Everyone has a right to live as comfortably as we do.

## Contrasts and Surprises

It is often true that the gap between the rich and poor countries is widening, although it depends on which countries are being compared. With the exception of some African nations, all countries in the Third World are progressing in terms of wealth. This provides small comfort for many, as the United Nations estimates that one billion people live on less than one (U.S.) dollar per day and that

800 million people are regularly hungry. The World Food Programme spent one million dollars a day in 1995 feeding the hungry, 70 percent of whom were women and children.

However, the news is not all bad, and we must acknowledge what has been achieved, especially since the Industrial Revolution began in Britain in the eighteenth century. Since that time, technology has enabled the living conditions of the poor to be improved. Before the Industrial Revolution, poverty was a brutal fact, accepted by the masses and tolerated or ignored by most of the rich minority. Churches rather than governments provided relief. Other factors, such as the rise of capitalism, the supremacy of market economies, the spread of democratic governments and the extension of education, have also contributed to this progress. Nevertheless, there is no reason to think that we have reached the limit of human ingenuity—new wonders will be produced in future generations, both for good and ill.

Progress is real. Between 1971 and 1995, in the low-income countries (e.g., China and India), infant mortality has been cut in half, life expectancy has risen by twelve years, secondary-school enrollments have doubled and clean water has been made available to an additional one billion people, at a time when the world population has increased by about two billion. Average real income per head in the developing world has almost doubled in this time. In the developing countries in the last twenty-five years, food production has also doubled and average nutritional intake has improved by at least 20 percent.

Indeed, the world today is producing more food than it needs. Some of it is destroyed, and there are huge stockpiles in Europe and the United States. The problem is distribution, not production. The fact that real wheat prices have been declining since 1900 is evidence of the abundance of supply.

Between 1979 and 1993, the Food and Agricultural Organization (FAO) published statistics that showed that food production per head throughout the world increased by 3 percent during that period. The general increase throughout Asia was 22 percent, with India showing a 23 percent increase and China a 39 percent increase.

Despite these advances, many people still require assistance. But there is evidence of "compassion fatigue", although hopefully it will only be temporary. In 1994, Official Development Assistance from donor countries dropped by a tenth worldwide and global food aid fell by almost 25 percent.

## Church Teaching

The Catholic Church recognizes the rights of governments, acting in the genuine interests of citizens, to monitor population numbers and encourage trends in growth or decline. However, governments have no right to use authoritarian, coercive measures.

Opinions differ about suitable levels of population for different countries. One opinion is that population growth needs to be restrained in some countries, such as India and China, but encouraged in others, such as Western Europe and Australia, always using appropriate moral means.

However, it is the spouses, husbands and wives, who have the first responsibility for the procreation and education of their children and should therefore make the decisions on the appropriate number and spacing of their babies.

The general Christian perspectives on marriage and family are quite clear. The sacrament of marriage, like holy orders, is a sacrament for others; husband and wife for each other and for the children. Marriage and family are at the service of life, of the next generation. A refusal to have any children is one ground for a marriage annulment by the Church.

Both Scripture and Catholic tradition see large families as a sign of God's blessing and parental generosity. Couples who are unable to have children suffer greatly.

Deciding the number and timing of children is a private and intimate matter for married couples, influenced by many different factors and determined ultimately by reasons that can be good and reasonable or plainly selfish.

Everywhere in the world, serious, or practicing, Catholics are recognized by the strength of their family life, even when the families are damaged and imperfect, and for the special place children are given.

Married love naturally tends to be fruitful. A baby is not an extra; not something from outside, but comes from the very heart of the couple's mutual love; the fruit and fulfillment of their union.

Pope Paul VI in 1968 repeated the constant teaching of the Church that "each and every marriage act must remain open to the transmission of life." This means that the Church believes in working with nature, respecting the natural rhythms of life, and is opposed to artificial contraception through the pill or sterilization or the use of condoms.

This is a hard teaching and has not been popular with many Catholics. However artificial contraception makes it easier for selfishness to take over, for a "contraceptive mentality" to triumph.

In the 1960s, as the pill became available, there was a lot of optimism that every child would now be wanted, that married life would be easier and happier, that the divorce rate would be lower, that abortions would be fewer—all because of the pill. None of this has happened; easy contraception has been accompanied, at least in the Western world, by a steady rise in the number of abortions.

Christians link together love-making and children within the institution of heterosexual marriage. Spouses share in the creative power and fatherhood of God. Every marriage act unites the spouses (unitive dimension) and should remain at least open to the possibility of life (procreative dimension).

Natural family planning requires periodic abstinence from sexual intercourse and self-discipline by the man as well as the woman. The Church does not believe that the woman should take all the responsibility for fertility, and the enthusiasm for regular use of the pill, with its chemical side effects on the woman, contrasts strongly with our modern antipathies to pollution, our sensitivities toward preserving the integrity of living organisms.

Selfishness does not make for happiness or good marriages, and artificial contraception can easily encourage too much "selfism".

●●●●●●●●●●●●●●●●●●●●●●●●●●●●●●●●●●●●●●●●●●

## *Bibliography*

*Catechism of the Catholic Church,* especially pt. 3, sec. 2, chap. 2, arts. 4 and 6, pars. 2196–2257, 2331–79.

The following sources were used to review the basic issues:

Ehrlich, Paul, *The Population Bomb* (1968).

Ehrlich, Paul, and Anne Ehrlich, *The Population Explosion* (1990).

Simon, Julian L., *Population Matters* (1990), 362–63.

The following sources were used to research the statistics quoted throughout this chapter:

*Bulletin Mensuel d'Information de l'Institut d'Études Démographiques,* August-September 1993, no. 282.

*New York Times,* September 8, 1994.

*Population Research Institute Review.*

Sen, Amartya, "Population: Delusion and Reality", *New York Review of Books* 22 (September 1994): 62–71.

*Statistical Abstracts,* pp. 7, 830.

United States Census Bureau, *Annual World Population Profile.*

United Nations, Food and Agricultural Organization, *FAO Quarterly Bulletin of Statistics.*

World Bank, *World Development Report,* OUP.

## For Review

1. Who are the writers warning of overpopulation? What are the facts?

2. What has happened with population estimates?

3. Has the Church expressed any view on population control? If so, summarize her stance on this issue.

4. Does a large population usually lead to poverty?

• • • • • • • • • • • • • • • • • • • • • • • • •

## Consider These

1. Who should make decisions about population growth in a country?

2. Find out what you can about China's "one child" policy and how it is being implemented.

3. Undertake a class survey of family sizes. Contrast your results with family sizes from one or two generations ago. Are there ethnic differences? Have changes in family size brought greater happiness?

4. Is it reasonable these days to want to have a large family? What factors would justify such a desire?

• • • • • • • • • • • • • • • • • • • • • • • • •

## Extension Exercises

1. Investigate the forms of Natural Family Planning. Why have they been more popular in Third World countries than elsewhere? Invite a guest speaker from an NFP team to address your class.

2. Invite a guest speaker to your school who has lived in a crowded Third World country. Question him on community life and on the relationship between poverty and happiness.

3. The English writer P. D. James, the "Agatha Christie" of our generation, has written a terrifying novel entitled *The Children of Men* (1992) about when the human race lost its power to breed. Can you even imagine a cursed world without children?

# CHAPTER FIFTEEN

# What Is Environmentalism?

*What can Catholics do to improve our environment?*

The media and class texts often warn us about the threats to planet earth from dangers such as industrial pollution, global warming, nuclear waste, acid rain and asbestos. Much of this worry is certainly warranted. However, is some of it connected with the decline in religious belief? Why are people who are sceptical about the existence of hell, or even heaven, often only too willing to believe extreme hypotheses about the next environmental disaster? People who believe God is good and that he has given us intelligence to help us through difficult times are usually slower to believe the worst. But environmental problems are real. What should we do? How do we obtain accurate information on these important issues? Do we have moral obligations environmentally? Has Christianity any useful perspectives to help us think about the environment?

## Varieties of Environmentalism

There are many varieties of Christianity—Catholicism, eastern Orthodoxy, Anglicanism, Protestantism—just as there are different types of environmentalism. The most moderate form of environmental ethics has gained widespread acceptance over the last twenty or thirty years. It recognizes God as the Creator who has given humans responsibilities toward all other living things (i.e., animals and plants). It teaches that natural resources are to be used wisely. Moderate environmentalists favor conservation, provided it is not too expensive or disruptive for humans. They also favor stewardship of the land and the preservation of endangered species. Their framework is anthropocentric ("man-centered"), and the environment is to be respected and managed for the benefit of the present and future generations. This is sometimes called "shallow" environmental ethics. However, consistent Christians belong in this category.

The next or "intermediate" stage of environmentalism denies the exclusive supremacy of humans over nature and denies that humanity is the measure of all things. The rights and duties considered as peculiar to human beings are to be extended to other species of animal and even plant life. So there is a "land ethic" and the animal liberation movement. It is interesting that these more extreme forms of environmental ethics flourish more in Australia than in any other country in the world.

In this second category of environmentalists is Professor Peter Singer, who is probably Australia's best known philosopher and a founder of the animal liberation movement. Singer denies the existence of God, denies any purpose to creation and certainly denies that humans are the centerpiece of all creation and destined for eternity. For him, such a claim is "speciesism".

154

There are other more extreme varieties of environmentalism—for example, differing strands of radical or "deep ecology" that unite to oppose the basic assumptions and socioeconomic structures of Western industrialized civilization (which is based on humanist and technological ideals). These groups denounce what they call "reformist, instrumentalist environmentalism", which seeks to reduce industrial pollution and use natural resources for the benefit of humanity. Many of these "deep ecologists" would like the human population to be only a fraction of what it is today, and they have a radical political agenda. The nature of this minority extremism is captured by the remark of one "deep-green" ecologist, Edward Abbey, who said that he would sooner shoot a man than a snake!

Yet others are "ecofeminists", who see the ecological crisis as the logical result of patriarchal domination (i.e., the domination and damage of the environment by rich and powerful men at the expense of the poor and powerless). According to these ecofeminists, when patriarchy is dismantled, both nature and human relations will be liberated. The public statements of some writers are extraordinary. For example, Carl Amery wants a "cultural model in which the killing of a forest will be considered more contemptible and more criminal than the sale of six-year-old children to Asian brothels".

Although the extremists are a minority, they are active propagandists. Many are anti-religious, indeed, probably the most active neopagans. Older pagans at least believed that life had a purpose. Most pagans today think that life is caused by chance and that there is no ultimate purpose or goal.

## God's Creation

The first solemn words of Sacred Scripture from the Old Testament Book of Genesis are: "In the beginning God created the heavens and the earth" (Genesis 1:1). This belief is restated by the Church when we pray the Apostles' Creed, where God is described as the "Creator of heaven and earth" and "of all that is, seen and unseen" (Nicene Creed). Therefore, the whole universe in its baffling immensity and mystery is not governed by blind chance or by anonymous necessity. Another consequence is that the universe had a beginning, perhaps synonymous with what modern science calls the "big bang", and exists for a purpose.

There is no everlasting wheel of return, as claimed in some Eastern religions, and God did not abandon his work immediately after creation, which shows his goodness, wisdom and glory. God is not like a watchmaker who made a watch, wound it up and left it to its devices (a theory called deism). The whole Trinity, Father, Son and Spirit, has always been involved in the common work of creation. As the late-second-century bishop of Lyons in France, Saint Irenaeus, wrote: "the glory of God is man fully alive", just as "man's life is the vision of God" (*Against the Heresies* 4.20.7).

Human beings have a special part in God's plan for creation, because to them was given the responsibility of subduing the earth and having dominion over it (Genesis 1:26–28). Men and women, acting freely and intelligently, are called to cooperate with God and complete the work of creation, to perfect its harmony for their own good and that of their neighbors. Often unknowingly, through their actions, prayers and sufferings, they become God's fellow workers, building up his kingdom.

The story of creation in the Bible is found basically in the first three chapters of Genesis. It does not give a scientific account of how God created the world. Therefore, many theologians believe that God probably did create the universe through some series of evolutionary changes and that the development of conscious life is the central, unique fact about this universe.

### The Imperfections of Nature

God's creation is good but imperfect. Evil and suffering are grim, sometimes terrible, realities. This fact is one important reason why Christians are not pantheists, who believe that everything is part of God. Christians do not worship nature because it is imperfect and sometimes dangerous and destructive. God is infinitely greater than all his works. As Saint Augustine of Hippo in North Africa (A.D. 354–430) wrote, God is "higher than my highest and more inward than my innermost self" (*Confessions* 3:6.11).

However, the existence of evil and suffering is the biggest problem for all monotheists (i.e., people who believe in the one true God). If God is good and all-powerful, why does he allow evil to flourish, not just in social structures, but in the human heart and in nature itself? Jews and Christians grapple with this problem using the doctrine of original sin.

We all know the story of the fall of Adam and Eve recounted in chapter three of Genesis. It gives a richly symbolic account of this primeval event when our first parents sinned and defied God by eating from the "tree of knowledge of good and evil" (Genesis 2:17). The tree is a symbol of the limits that all men must recognize and respect. When we try to make ourselves like gods, we pay the penalty. Scripture tells us of the tragic consequences of this first disobedience. Our first parents lost the grace of original holiness and developed a distorted image of God, whom they feared. Their son Cain murdered his brother Abel. Many in history have since burned the brand of Cain into their souls. Death has come into our story.

There is now a flaw in the human heart: the relationships of men and women are subject to tension and often marked by lust and domination. The original harmony is also destroyed within creation, which has become alien to man and subject to inevitable decay. Adam was condemned to battle against brambles and thistles and to produce his food with great difficulty, "with sweat on . . . [his] brow", until his death. "For dust you are and to dust you shall return" (Genesis 3:17–19).

It is not difficult to believe in the doctrine of original sin because there is so much evidence for evil and suffering in history and in nature itself. We recognize this often when we speak of the natural world, in which the "law of the jungle" reigns supreme. Scientists have written of the survival of the fittest; of the triumph of the selfish gene. We know of the food chain, where the balance of nature is maintained as one species feeds off another. We also know of the cruelty of animals and of their instinct to hunt. Even the most domesticated cat is transformed by the prospect of catching a bird or tormenting a mouse. Nature is also implacable. Remember, God always forgives, man sometimes forgives, but nature never forgives. Evidence abounds for this.

If we drink enough alcohol, our livers will be damaged, just as lung cancer may follow smoking and venereal disease may accompany promiscuity. Similarly, if we destroy too many trees, erosion often occurs; when whole forests are destroyed, rainfall can be drastically diminished. Industrial discharges have produced acid rain across much of Europe.

Nature is wonderful and spectacular; often mysterious, but it is not always benign. It is an important sign or sacrament of God's greatness—but brush fires, floods, volcanoes and typhoons are also part of the picture. Nature should be respected, but it makes a poor object for worship and an inferior substitute for religious awe. The yearning for a vanished Arcadia and the ideal of the noble savage are based on a barren, misleading myth.

## Useful Perspectives

It is not the task of the Catholic Church, nor that of any other religious body, to lay down specific guidelines to protect the environment. This is the task of our elected leaders, the politicians, after they have evaluated the studies of the scientists and considered the costs (financial and otherwise) in the light of the requirements of social justice.

The Church has no special scientific competence. Her task is to spell out the moral imperatives necessary for the integrity of creation to be respected. The mineral, vegetable and animal resources of the universe are to be used for the common good of present and future generations. Therefore, our dominion is not absolute but subservient to the good of all humanity.

Animals are to be treated with kindness because they are God's creatures. It is sinful to cause them to suffer or die needlessly. However, as animals are entrusted to human stewardship, they can be domesticated as helpmates and used to produce food and clothing. Scientific experimentation on animals, within reasonable limits, is also acceptable when it contributes to the development of medicine.

Democratic government and a free press are the best defenders of the environment: free media can spell out when people and the countryside are being endangered; a government that is truly representative of the people will respond to popular pressures. The terrible environmental damage that can result from an absence of these two elements is well known. It was displayed in Ukraine when the Chernobyl nuclear reactor exploded in 1986. In Russia the huge and once beautiful Aral Sea is now half its former size because of irrigation programs. In 1965 the life expectancy for men in the USSR was sixty-six years; in 1994 it was sixty-one. The Russian birthrate has dropped alarmingly. In 1994, there were 700,000 more deaths than births. Rivers, forests, tundra and people's health have been destroyed. The Arctic Ocean was used as a nuclear dump. There are many pockets of zinc, lead and sulphur, all of which are poisonous and have caused respiratory troubles, birth defects and high rates of cancer.

Blatant examples like this are not difficult to recognize, although the economic costs to remedy such situations will be enormous for many years. It is more difficult to discover the truth about long-term, hidden dangers, especially as the scientists often differ among themselves.

Educated men and women learn to be sceptical toward even the most highly regarded books; certainly toward newspapers and television shows, which often reduce complicated issues to a "sound-bite" of a few minutes. We too should want to test the evidence and examine the lines of argument and to be at least as demanding and discriminating when considering scientific evidence, especially on health and the environment, where there are often powerful, vested interests at play that employ their own publicity departments to influence public opinion on conservation.

The answers to environmental problems lie in better applications of science, industry and technology, not in a return to the Middle Ages or something even more simple and remote. Going "back to nature" would be unhealthy and uncomfortable. Science has given us the atomic bomb, but this is an exception among a multitude of blessings. The Industrial Revolution produced terrible slums, but it also enabled more people than ever before to escape from poverty. There are so many things we now take for granted and which we regard as basic necessities, such as health care,

159

schooling, electricity, heating, the automobile and television. Such "basic necessities" are only possible because of science and technology. There is a down-side, negative consequences such as pollution and the ability to manufacture incredibly destructive weapons of war, but the pluses far outweigh the minuses.

## Global Warming?

A brief history of the conflicting and changing scientific advice on the problem of global warming due to the "greenhouse effect" (the increase of carbon dioxide, methane and nitrous oxide in the atmosphere) is indicative of the difficulties of obtaining accurate information about the past and projecting trends into the future. Without the "greenhouse effect", the earth would be 50°F colder and life as we know it could not exist.

At the United Nations earth summit at Rio de Janeiro in 1992, a strong consensus that the dangers to the environment were real led to the creation of the 1992 Rio Framework Convention on Climate Change.

Government enthusiasm, however, had waned considerably by the 1995 UNO Berlin conference on climate. Governments were more sceptical and cautious, perhaps because the drastic shortages of food and energy forecast in the 1970s had not come about. In addition, Third World governments were suspicious that the West was opposing their industrial development and that Western environmental groups seemed to value the preservation of forests and landscapes in poor countries above the needs of the people themselves.

While all seemed to agree that the amount of carbon dioxide in the atmosphere had increased by about 25 to 30 percent since 1750, opinions still varied about whether the world's average temperature had risen and how much sea levels might rise as a result.

Greenpeace claims that the decade before 1994 was the hottest on record. New accurate satellite-derived temperature readings for 1980 to 1993 showed no global warming over that period. The Intergovernmental Panel on Climate Control (established by the World Meteorological Office) estimated heating of 0.75 degrees during the previous one hundred years in their document *Climate Change 1992.*

Another hypothesis was that global warming would melt large sections of the Antarctic ice sheet and that sea levels would rise. In 1980 some scientists said sea levels would rise by twenty-six feet over the next century. In 1989 scientists said sea levels would rise by three feet. In 1990 two feet was the estimate, provided the global temperature rose by seven degrees. In 1993, one authority estimated that the sea level would rise eight inches in a century if carbon dioxide levels quadrupled, but the effects of melting ice were impossible to predict.

The 1995 IPPC report claims that recent unusual weather patterns have been caused by human activity and distinguishes temperature levels of near surface air (0.5–1°F rise since late last century), of troposphere and of stratosphere where the temperature dropped one degree between 1979 and 1984. It predicts a sea level rise of between six and thirty-eight inches by the year 2100.

In about 1980 the media and scientists such as Doctor Steve Schneider of the U.S. (by 1995 a global warming fan) were warning the world about the dangers of a new Ice Age!

The ice has advanced nine times in the last 850,000 years. Each intermission or interglacial has lasted between 10,000 to 20,000 years. Ours started about 14,000 years ago. Our long-term successors are more likely to find themselves in the refrigerator than the furnace!

We should not be surprised by these conflicts and changes over time in the different branches of science. Human knowledge advances in this way. Furthermore, predicting the future is a particularly hazardous business for everyone.

*Bibliography*

*Catechism of the Catholic Church*, especially pt. 1, sec. 2, chap. 1, art. 1, par. 4, 279–324.

Singer, Peter, *Spectator*, September 16, 1995, 22.

Anderson, Kenneth, and Robert Wokler, "Ecology: A Deeper Shade of Green", *Times Literary Supplement*, September 8, 1995, 9–15.

●●●●●●●●●●●●●●●●●●●●●●●●

*For Review*

1. What are some of the different ethical theories concerning the environment?

2. Why should Christians be concerned about the environment, and how concerned should they be?

●●●●●●●●●●●●●●●●●●●●●●●●

*Consider These*

1. Consider the cartoon below. What issues are addressed in it?

2. Gather together several articles from newspapers about the environment. Identify the main concerns being addressed in

each article. Are these concerns justified? Can you identify any interest groups?

3. Jobs or the environment: Which is more important?

4. Is environmental disaster just around the corner? Here? Elsewhere?

5. A 1995 survey of young Australian secondary-school students claimed that there was less interest than there had been in the past in religious beliefs but more concern about the environment. Is this true of your class? Of you?

6. Are God and the environment alternatives?

## Extension Exercises

1. Nature and the universe sometimes inspire beautiful music. Listen to excerpts from Antonio Vivaldi's (1678–1741) *Four Seasons*, the Austrian Joseph Haydn's 1798 oratorio *The Creation*; and the Russian Igor Stravinsky's (1882–1971) *The Rite of Spring*. Listen to each piece. What ideas does each of them express about the environment? How are those ideas and music expressed?

2. Saint Francis of Assisi (1181–1226) is one of the Catholic Church's most memorable saints. A deacon, never a priest, he was the founder of the Franciscan orders. The following hymn, written by Saint Francis and entitled "Canticle of Brother Sun", praises the work of the one true God in creation and represents an important development in Christian theology.

> Most High, all-powerful, good Lord,
> Yours are the praises, the glory, the honor, and all
> blessing.

To You alone, Most High, do they belong
and no man is worthy to mention Your name.
Praised be You, my Lord, with all Your creatures,
especially Sir Brother Sun,
Who is the day and through whom You give us light.
And he is beautiful and radiant with great splendor
and bears a likeness of You, Most High One.
Praised be You, my Lord, through Sister Moon and the
    stars,
In heaven You formed them clear and precious and
    beautiful.
Praised be You, my Lord, through Brother Wind,
and through the air, cloudy and serene, and every kind of
    weather
through which You give sustenance to Your creatures.
Praised be You, my Lord, through Sister Water,
which is very useful and humble and precious and chaste,
Praised be You, my Lord, through Brother Fire,
through whom You light the night
and he is beautiful and playful and robust and strong.
Praised be You, my Lord, through our Sister Mother Earth,
who sustains and governs us
and who produces varied fruits with colored flowers and
    herbs.

Do you believe that this is a suitable prayer for our age? Would
you use it to praise God and thank him for the beauties of creation?

3. The English priest Gerard Manley Hopkins (1844–1889) is one
of the founders of modern poetry. He wrote the following poem,
entitled "God's Grandeur":

The world is charged with the grandeur of God.
It will flame out, like shining from shook foil;
It gathers to a greatness, like the ooze of oil
Crushed. Why do men then now not reck his rod?

Generations have trod, have trod, have trod;
And all is seared with trade; bleared, smeared with toil;
And wears man's smudge and shares man's smell: the soil
Is bare now, nor can foot feel, being shod.

And for all this, nature is never spent;
There lives the dearest freshness deep down things;
And though the last lights off the black West went
Oh, morning, at the brown brink eastward, springs—
Because the Holy Ghost over the bent
World broods with warm breast and with ah! bright wings.

a. Describe the images of the world given in this poem.

b. What does the poem suggest about mankind's treatment of nature?

c. Explain what is meant by "There lives the dearest freshness deep down things."

d. Do you find God in creation? Often? Easily?


4. The nineteenth-century English novelist Charles Dickens wrote powerfully about the sufferings of the poor in British industrial slums. Have you read *David Copperfield* or *Oliver Twist*? Are there slums in our country today like those described in Dickens' books? Are there such slums elsewhere?

# CHAPTER SIXTEEN

# Death: An End or a New Beginning?

*What is your attitude toward death?*
*What is heaven like?*

Death is mysterious and different. Some die peacefully and are prepared for death; some die suddenly and unexpectedly; others die with violence. The following scenarios provide examples of this variety.

A man who was in his seventies died at home after years of sickness and suffering but surrounded by his wife and family and strengthened by prayers and sacraments. He remembered a life of goodness and achievement and kept his sense of humor to the end. His was a beautiful death.

A young married woman was killed with her two preschool daughters in a traffic accident while taking lunch to her husband on the farm. The unborn baby she was carrying was also killed. Theirs was a tragic death.

Why are life and death so different and unpredictable? What comes after death? Where is God's hand in this?

## Death

A sprightly seventy-year-old woman tells how, when she retired, she was often asked what she was going to do. "Enjoy myself and prepare for death", she always replied, to the discomfort of most of her hearers. Most people choose to avoid what is generally considered to be a morbid topic unless it is unavoidable. Death is a shadow over each of us, seen as a distant threat rather than the gateway to eternal life. We know our loved ones cannot live forever and neither can we. An old music hall song used to declare, "Everybody wants to go to heaven, but nobody wants to die."

Nearly everyone is at least a little frightened of death and of passing into the great unknown, although nature has arranged it that very few young people have a preoccupation with dying—death happens to other people, and later! As people grow older, attitudes toward death change, although there is an immense variety of approaches. The presence or absence of religious faith can make a huge difference. Pagans (who do not believe in the one true God) often take the attitude, "Eat, drink and be merry for tomorrow we die." Health, beauty and perpetual youth are idolized, old age is regretted and not respected, and the sick and elderly are often locked out of sight in nursing homes and hospitals and rarely visited. A few people even say that society should save money and resources by committing euthanasia, or "mercy killing", of such human "encumbrances". After all, rising health costs are a national problem.

The great religions differ from each other, but all religious people have attitudes toward death that are distinct from those of pagans. Christians want to die well. A good death (with dignity and faith) is a worthwhile human achievement, like a good marriage or the successful rearing of children. And for Christians, death is not the end. The Christian attitude toward suffering is also different. For many pagans, suffering is not just difficult and sometimes terrible: it actually has no meaning and is treated only as a brutal fact. For Christians, the Cross on which the Son of God died is also a symbol of redemption, a pointer to the resurrection. We can join our sufferings to Christ's and turn them to good, asking God to use them for some good purpose.

No other group has battled as hard and as long against suffering as the Christians. There were Christian hospitals long before there were government hospitals. All Christians are called to practice compassion (which means curing, caring and not killing). Death is believed to be an entry to life, that is, a different kind of life.

## Eternal Life

In 1993 Pope John Paul II began one of his most important encyclicals (titled *Veritatis Splendor*) on the basics of the Church's moral teaching with a meditation on the rich young man who asked our Lord, "Teacher, what good must I do to have eternal life?" (Matthew 19:16–22). This is not a question much asked today, but it should be. What is more important than our final and eternal destination? Like most of us, the young man believed in heaven, although the Jews of his time differed about the resurrection of the body, accepted by the Pharisees but rejected by the Sadducees.

As in many areas, Jesus' teaching on life after death is built on Jewish doctrines. He regularly taught about heaven and hell, which are the eternal states of reward or punishment for the good or evil performed during our individual lives. For our Lord, heaven is a complete answer to our deepest human longings. It brings an end to our sadness and healing to our hurts. It will still our restlessness and remove our fears and worries. As Saint Paul claimed, "no eye has seen, nor ear has heard, nor the heart of man conceived, what God has prepared for those who love him" (1 Corinthians 2:9). Heaven brings supreme, definitive happiness to each individual, probably enjoyed according to our differing personal capacities, just as people enjoy the same leisure activities in different ways.

Faith and good works are the criteria for entry to heaven. Experience tells each of us that some are better persons than others. An extreme example proves this fact: none of us would claim to be as good a person as Mary, the Mother of our Savior; all of us would hope to commit less evil than Hitler and Stalin. We should not be surprised then to find in heaven that each of us sees God as he is and fully enjoys the fruits of the redemption achieved by Christ on the Cross according to the capacity for loving we have each developed before death. We shall continue as persons, finding our true identity, by being with Christ, the Son of God, by living in Christ (Philippians 1:23).

In our culture today the word "heaven" is a bit like the word "devil"—both words conjure up many misleading images. The spirit of evil that flared unchecked under Pol Pot, in Rwanda and Bosnia, and during the Holocaust is not expressed in any useful way by a mischievous little fellow with a tail and a pitchfork. Similarly, the popular version of heaven, with its baroque images of angel choirs, clouds of glory, harps, organ music and fat cherubs, distracts and even hinders us from developing an accurate (even if still limited) understanding of what heaven is about.

The Scripture images of heaven may be divided into two families. The first uses earthly delights like those found in an earthly paradise—the wedding feast, the heavenly Jerusalem, the wine of the kingdom, the Father's house. The second line of thought, favored also by the mystics, speaks of life, peace and especially of light and overwhelming love. All our language of eternity is inadequate, but the Scripture terminology is not misleading. It points us in the right direction. During the past two thousand years of Christian history, theologians and saints have filled out the gaps in the scriptural evidence on heaven in differing ways—but there have been no heresies about heaven.

For all Christians, heaven is God-centered. People throughout history have differed about the nature and importance of relationships in heaven with loved ones, about whether we shall be able to do things, about the nature of our risen bodies and of the new heaven and earth. For example, the Gothic cathedrals of the twelfth to sixteenth centuries (such as Notre Dame in Paris and Salisbury Cathedral in Britain, painted so beautifully by John Constable and J. M. W. Turner) are characterized by light-filled stained-glass windows and soaring spires. The circular rose windows in these buildings were designed to symbolize the perfection of God, radiating brilliant streams of love and light. Their architectural style embodies one theology of heaven.

## Judgment

There is not a great distance between an easy assumption that everyone goes to heaven and a later conclusion that heaven is only a consoling myth for the simple-minded. Often what is missing in both of these approaches is any consideration of the problems of evil and human suffering. To such a consideration, some might reply that entry to heaven is a human right that God owes to us all, just as other people must respect our right to life or our right to vote. However, this attitude does not grapple with the problem that many victims die before receiving justice and that some monstrous criminals seem to enjoy a long and pleasurable life.

If the one true God is good and all-powerful, then logic would seem to require that the scales of justice balance out in eternity, just as certainly as they do not always balance out for individuals before death. An individual judgment for each person is necessary. In fact, this is Christian teaching. The Church follows Christ our Lord in teaching that each person immediately after death is rewarded according to the quality of his faith and life. In this life it is never too late to repent. Indeed, final repentance is always possible, as Christ's promise on the Cross to the "good" thief who died with him shows (Luke 23:43). However, through this particular judgment every individual gains entrance to the blessedness of heaven, either immediately or through the purification of purgatory, or is condemned to everlasting damnation.

Scripture also tells us that Christ will come again "in his glory and all the angels with him" to separate the good from the evil, to divide the entire human race "into the sheep on his right and the goats on his left, the righteous into eternal light and the wicked into eternal punishment" (Matthew 25:31–46; John 5:25–29; Acts 24:15). The resurrection of all the dead, just and unjust, will precede the Last Judgment. Christ's return was such a vivid expectation for some of the first Christians that Saint Paul had to warn the Thessalonians to stick to their jobs no matter how soon Christ's Second Coming might or might not be! This is one mistake we are not tempted to make.

Christians believe, not just in the continuing existence of each individual soul, but that the resurrection of our bodies on the last day will be accompanied by a mysterious renewal of the entire universe. There will be a "new heaven and a new earth", when God's plan for all history and creation has been fulfilled, the work of the kingdom finally completed and the mysterious ways of providence revealed. Love and justice will have the last word, and death will be conquered. Christ will be revealed as the omega point, the end and explanation of all creation. The plan hidden from the beginning will expose everything, brought "together under Christ as head, everything in the heavens and everything on earth" (Ephesians 1:9–10).

The purification of the imperfect, which will occur before the Last Judgment, will take place in purgatory. The word "purgatory" is not a scriptural term but is an age-old Christian belief, expressed in the ancient customs of offering Mass and praying for the dead and founded on the passage from the Old Testament Second Book of Maccabees (12:45), where Judas Maccabeus "had this atonement sacrifice offered for the dead [his soldiers], so that they might be released from their sin". Since it is not difficult to imagine ourselves unready for the beatific vision (that is, the presence of God), the existence of purgatory presents no logical problems. People often admit that they are not yet ready for marriage; that they need to do more study before they can pass an exam or that they are not yet expert enough to play in a particular team or band. So too with meeting God.

Some people do their purgatory on earth through their sufferings. This is not true for everyone. One writer explained purgatory as being where the soul after death finds its equilibrium. The saint can cope with God's pure light and love, the sinner heads for the darkness, while the imperfect are uncomfortable because our imperfections and faults are laid bare and appear hideous in comparison with God's perfection. Our pride is wounded when we see the truth, until we are liberated through love and forgiveness. Purgatory is God's demanding, purifying love.

The Catholic tradition of praying for the dead at their funerals, on the anniversary of their deaths and especially around All Souls Day on November 2 is therefore important. In addition, it will probably be useful for each of us later!

## Hell

Many Christians have some difficulty with the idea of hell, an eternity of punishment, because it is hard to reconcile with the goodness and love of God. However, there is more in the Scriptures about hell than there is about purgatory. The Church follows Christ in teaching that hell exists, but there is no Church teaching that any person is certainly in hell. We cannot even be sure of the fate of Judas Iscariot, who betrayed our Lord.

Jesus often spoke of "Gehenna" (the "unquenchable fire") reserved for those who refused to believe and be converted. The final division recounted in chapter twenty-five of Matthew's Gospel has already been mentioned, which includes Christ's terrible, ultimate condemnation: "Depart from me, you cursed, into the eternal fire" (Matthew 25:41). We have no right to reject this teaching of Christ and the Church simply because we regard it as too fierce or too unpleasant. We have even less right to reject it if neither we nor our loved ones have suffered badly at the hands of some unrepentant criminal. Crime and proper punishment together constitute a great mystery, even in eternity. We must always remember that Christ, the just judge who balances the scales, is the second Person of the Trinity. He predestines no one to hell and does not want "any to perish, but all to come to repentance" (2 Peter 3:9). God is not cruel or capricious or relentless. God is infinitely more loving and forgiving than the best human father or mother. But God respects human freedom: he is powerless before a human refusal to repent and must deliver justice to the victims.

Our Lord spoke of the eternal fires of hell. Others have spoken of utter darkness, the absence of meaning, isolation, loneliness and terror, where pride prevents repentance and suicide is not a possibility. Young children should not be threatened with hell, but young adults should be aware of scriptural teaching on hell, just as they must also come to terms with the prospect of dying, the significance of health risks, the existence of examinations and the necessity for study.

During times of intense prayer (as in a retreat), Catholics are encouraged to meditate on the four last things: death, judgment, heaven and hell. But we approach each differently. We know we shall die. We expect to be judged, and consequently we hope for heaven and fear hell. It is for this reason that Catholics pray that God will not take them in death, suddenly and unprepared.

Some great Christian thinkers, even as early as Origen from Alexandria in Egypt in the third century, have dared to hope that even the most terrible moral monsters will eventually be purified through suffering for heaven. Perhaps they are right, although the Church has never approved this theory. We must leave these things to our loving, forgiving and just God, remembering the words of the old hymn:

> There's a wideness in God's mercy
> which is wider than the sea.

• • • • • • • • • • • • • • • • • • • • • • • • •

## Bibliography

*Catechism of the Catholic Church,* especially pt. 1, sec. 2, arts. 11–12, pars. 988–1060.

Pope John Paul II, *Veritatis Splendor* (1993).

*For Review*

1. What do Christians believe about the Last Judgment?

2. What do we know about life after death?

3. What does purgatory mean?

*Consider These*

1. Have you ever been to a funeral? Was the service appropriate? What elements make a difference (for better or for worse)?

2. a. Why is there a taboo on discussing death and dying in our society?

   b. To whom would you talk if a close friend or relative of yours died?

3. Go for a walk through a local cemetery and read some of the tombstones. What thoughts do they provoke?

4. Think of some of the advertisements for funeral services on television. Is death being commercialized?

5. What do you think heaven will be like?

6. Do you think some people might deserve hell?

*Extension Exercises*

1. Listen to the dramatic concert piece *The Damnation of Faust,* by the French composer Hector Berlioz (1803–1869). Does it capture something of the pandemonium of hell? What about Berlioz' "March to the Scaffold" from his *Symphonie Fantastique?*

2. Saint Ambrose was a provincial governor in the Roman Empire who became bishop of Milan in northern Italy in A.D. 374. A great writer and preacher, he is one of the four Doctors (or greatest teachers) in Western Christianity, along with Saint Augustine, Saint Jerome and Pope Saint Gregory the Great. He wrote the following on the blessing of death.

> The Lord allowed death to make its way into our world so that guilt should come to an end; but lest human nature should perish by death, he arranged for the resurrection of the dead.
>
> Death in this sense is a pilgrimage, a lifetime's pilgrimage that none must shirk, a pilgrimage from decay to imperishable life, from mortality to immortality, from anxiety to unruffled calm. Do not be afraid of the word death: rather rejoice in the blessings that follow a happy death. What's death after all but the burial of vice, the flowering of goodness.

Do you think your faith would ever be strong enough for you to think of death as Ambrose did? Are Ambrose's thoughts challenging and comforting?

3. Poet James McAuley became a Catholic in 1952 after having undertaken a long search for the truth. He wrote the following poem, entitled "Explicit", in 1976 when he left the hospital to go home to die from cancer.

> So the word has come at last:
> The argument of arms is past.
> Fully tested I've been found
> Fit to join the underground.
>
> Soon I'll understand it all,
> Or cease to wonder: so my small
> Spark will blaze intensely bright,
> Or go out in an endless night.
>
> Welcome now to bread and wine:
> Creature comfort, heavenly sign.

Winter will grow dark and cold
Before the wattle turns to gold.

Is there hope in this poem? Do you think it reveals the struggle
that McAuley underwent to find faith?